A MAN LIKE GOD

A MAN LIKE GOD

AS HE IS SO ARE WE

JAMES CRAIG

KINGDOM TRUTH
Atlanta, GA

All Scripture quotations are taken from the King James Version of the Holy Bible.

A MAN LIKE GOD
As He Is, So Are We
Trade paperback edition

James Craig
Atlanta, GA 30313
www.raisingkingdomcitizens.org

ISBN-13: 978-0692262078 • ISBN-10: 0692262075
Printed in the United States of America
© 2014 by James Craig

Kingdom Truth
369 McDaniel Street SW, Suite: 2604
Atlanta, GA 30313
kingdomtruth@mail.com

Library of Congress Control Number: 2014947087

No part of this book may be reproduced or transmitted in any form or by any means electronic or mechanical—including photocopying, recording, or by any information storage and retrieval system—without permission in writing from the publisher. Please direct your inquiries to permissioneditor@mail.com.

Table of Contents

Foreword 11
  My Prayer 12
Introduction 15
  Man's Image and Reputation 16
  The Spirit of Man 17
Chapter 1: The Man: Created 19
  The Creation 20
    Signs of Life 21
    Have Dominion 22
  Kingdom Order 22
  The Commandment 24
    The Benefits 24
  Created Man 26
Chapter 2: The Man: His Wo-Man 27
  Eve 27
    The Softer Side of Man 29
  The Unbreakable Covenant 29
  Marriage 30
  Sexual Immorality of Men and Absent Fathers . 32
  Husband's Role in Marriage 34
    No Divorce Clause 35
  The Marriage Bed Defiled 38

    The Spirit of Lust 40

    It is God to be Virgins 41

    Marry A Virgin.. 44

        Reestablishing the Sanctity of Virginity 46

Chapter 3: The Man: Fallen 51

    Sin and Death Interrupts Paradise 53

    The Kingdom Stolen 54

        The Glory has Departed............................. 56

    Our Adversary 58

        Tools of The Adversary 61

    Adam Where Are You?................................... 73

Chapter 4: The Man: Without God 75

    Plays The Fool.. 76

    Is Self-Willed.. 79

    Worships Strange Gods 82

Chapter 5: The Man: Child 85

    The Promise of A Son 86

    The Blood Speaks... 90

    The Molding of A Man 92

        The Nature of God.................................... 92

        An Adverse Nature.................................... 94

    God's Child Rearing Plan 97

    Come Out From Among Them...................... 100

Chapter 6: Man 103

    The Formative Years....................................... 104

    Men After Our Own Kind 106

    Is Spirit Not Flesh 108

        Image and Likeness of God...................... 109

    Identity Crisis 111

        The Bottom Line 113

Chapter 7: Man: In Crisis 115

    Prideful 117

    Wrath, Anger and Un-forgiveness 119

    The Original Plan 121

        Reestablishing The Original Plan 122

Chapter 8: In Need of A Savior 125

    Reason For A Savior 126

        Lost Connection With the Father 127

        Needs Something More 128

    Salvation's Plan 129

        The Misuse of Salvation........................... 131

    Salvation's Gift 134

        Restored Authority 134

        Power with Jesus.................................... 135

Chapter 9: Man Resurrected 139

    Alive From The Dead 140

        Free From Death.................................... 141

    The Unbelief of Believers............................ 143

    Awakened From Sleep 146

        Alive yet Perpetrating Death 148

Chapter 10: The Man: Jesus 151
   As He Is So Are We 153
      We are As He Is: Powerful 156
   Cornerstone of the Church 161

Chapter 11: Authority with Christ 163
   Working With The Lord 164
      Assignment 165
   Spiritual Authority 169
      Understanding Spiritual Matters 170
   The Tongue 172
      Double Tongue 173

Chapter 12: The Man Like God 175
   No Excuses 175
   Born of truth 176
   Cannot Sin 177
      Capacity to Sin 179
   Freely Expresses Love 181
   Faithful 183

Appendix 189
   Glossary 191

About The Author 195

FOREWORD

Growing up, I was taught subliminally by my peers, television and the men in my life; that being a man meant having lots of money, girls, a nice car and the ability to fight.

For some reason when I did not possess these things, I felt less than a man. My self-esteem, identity and manhood were codependent and measured by having these things. It wasn't until years later in my adulthood I discovered I'd been misinformed.

When I came naked before God my manufacturer, He not only cleared up all misconceptions about who I am, but also revealed to me my purpose as a man. Even today, many men, young and old are distracted in pursuing a false allusion of what he thinks a man is.

Can you imagine what this world would be like if all men took their rightful place in their families and churches, not just naturally but also spiritually? I thank God for all of the women of God, who have stood in the gap, but it's time for men to step up and accept the invitation to be a man who walks after the likeness of God.

"For the earnest expectation of the creature waiteth for the manifestation of the sons of God."

-*Romans 8:19*

The whole world waits in expectation of seeing the day God's glory is fully manifested in the lives of men:

A Man Like God

Some issues will not be corrected until men accept the challenge and invitation to be more like God.

I am excited about James Craig's new book, "**A Man Like God**." It is designed to help you as a man, young or old to understand your God-given value. Contrary to what we've been taught, James dispels all stigma's and stereotypes placed on men by revealing that a godly father, husband and son is attainable through Christ.

After reading this book, you will begin to discover your true identity in Christ. I picture this work helping men of all ages and ethnicities all around the world, empowering them to move forward in the things of God.

Are you ready to be the man God designed you to be? Do you desire to be a man who walks in the likeness of God?

Well, this book helps you to do just that. As you read through these pages prayerfully study the passages of scriptures shared and by so studying, your life will forever be changed.

My Prayer

Father God, I come to you as humble as I know how. I pray every man who comes in contact with this book, your Word and the Spirit of God will forever alter their lives. Open their minds and understanding. Cause men to see who you've created them to be.

I bind the works of Satan which has been formed against his life. I hereby render him powerless in the name of Jesus.

FOREWORD

Father I ask you to catapult this man into his destiny. Use him for your glory. Create in him a godly father, husband, son, and businessman this world so desperately needs, in the mighty name of Jesus, Amen (So Be It)!

~Pastor Kevin Hardin~

"All the ways of a man are clean in his own eyes; but the LORD weigheth the spirits." (Proverbs 16:2)

INTRODUCTION

There is a spirit of deception which has gone out to devalue men, to cause individuals to devalue the status of the man in his home, and in his community, so he has less value within himself. If he retains less value within himself, it is easy for him to believe the lies that the enemy perpetrates against him. It becomes easy to believe that no one loves him, or no one cares.

He then begins to seek value from drugs, sex, gangs, and other things that falsely makes him feel valued; which only proves to degrade him even more, and cause him to feel less than who he is, or was created.

Furthermore, man sought his manliness from amongst other failed men, or their manhood has been molded by women who are single mothers, and based on their own wounds and hurts attempted to mold their son into the image of a man they desired or wanted for themselves.

This left man fragmented within himself seeking recognition, acceptance, and love from those who are also fragmented and broken.

Society has given their concept of what is believed to be a man. What he should be how he should respond, and to deviate from any of their standards or status quo of what a man should be, is to risk ridicule.

However, all which have been described was developed through years of pressure, manipulation, and degradation of that which man was created to be.

A Man Like God

The image of manliness is created in sex, lies, and hypocrisy taken from a nature not his own, yet embraced as his own identity. Therefore, he is for the most part unstable, unfaithful, and seemingly unable to be trusted in relationships.

If he is faithful, truthful, and compassionate, he is seen as an exception and not the rule. Man has been downgraded to dogs, rats, and the filth of the earth and has for the most part embraced these references to himself; not understanding that none of these characteristics is whom he was created to be.

Man's Image and Reputation

Man embraced the image and taken on a reputation built upon him through the centuries. He has not deviated, or changed his stance through all his history, except to deny his true nature, and the God who created him.

Even those who have embraced Christ, and received the Spirit of God, embrace the lies society has placed on men, and perpetrated rape, molestations, homosexuality, adultery, and promiscuity in the midst of the congregation, and made the convenient excuse: "I am a man."

Men who proudly proclaim: "if a woman takes off her clothes in front of me, I am going to do what a man does (meaning he will have sex with her, even if married or otherwise committed)." Understanding neither what he says nor whereof he affirms his masculinity; for if he did, he would not foolishly proclaim such nonsense and take Joseph's example of running for his life (see Genesis 39:12).

INTRODUCTION

Man's false reputation has left him destitute and naked not knowing his true heritage, or his true origins. Therefore, because he does not know who he is, or where he comes from he chooses the lowest estate of his existence, and continues down the road of his demise; while boasting in his uprising falsely.

For his earthly reputation he will hurt, demean, and murder and yet proclaim himself man. He will beat down and step over his brother only to lift up himself and this also he says is the way of man.

However, the truth of man is hidden within him, which cries to be released, and to introduce himself to the person he's tucked away even from himself.

THE SPIRIT OF MAN

Hidden away in the deep recesses of his spirit is the true identity of a man; his true nature, his complete self, having no part missing, with the DNA of God the Father, who created him locked deep inside of him.

However, he ignores this and turns away from his true identity and denies it with all gravity. But the DNA of God trapped inside of him screams to see life and light again.

The soul of man created in the image and likeness of God the Father, and being held captive by the flesh of man; desires to be free by the Spirit of God, in order to embrace the face of his Father once again.

As a prince who left the comfort of the King's domain, living among the peasants of the kingdom eating filth and the refuse of the nobles, of which he once was privy to. So man has deviated from God and is

A MAN LIKE GOD

trapped in sin and death when he was created in life and true holiness.

Having embraced the lies of a dead kingdom and its master Satan, and having established himself through the nature of this same master; the soul of man has been left for dead.

However, the true master sent his son to revive, redeem, and restore the soul to his rightful place and stance in his true Kingdom. The Son of God destroyed the lies of sin and death, and made it possible for man to once again behold His presence.

What are you waiting on? Embrace the Father, and all he has for you, and receive the knowledge of who you are, whose you are, and who you are in His presence.

This book is written to confront, challenge, and raise men to their rightful place in the earth, and with the Father.

To reveal man's true nature to men, and debunk, debase, and flat out denounce the lies perpetrated by the devil to keep a men locked in a state that is not his own.

To sever the ties to sin, death, and lies, and present men to whom their true nature and God is.

Through the pages of this book, man comes face to face with the man he is, and becomes all he was meant to be; **A MAN LIKE GOD**.

Chapter 1

THE MAN: CREATED

"What is man that you are mindful of him? You have made him a little lower than yourself, crowned him with glory, has given him dominion over the works of your hand, and have put all things under his feet."

~Psalms 8, with emphasis added

Oh, how I wish it were in us to understand the things God has placed in the reach of man; to understand His thoughts in wanting something so close to Himself, so intimate, so personal, so loved.

Why would a God, who created everything and can create anything for His pleasure, create a being that has become so crass and disrespectful? For that matter, why would parents delight in producing a child who may one-day ostracize, criticize, curse, and demean them?

No doubt it is the joy parents receive from embracing something that is formed from their own flesh. For the man it's the joy of looking upon his son which issued from his own loins, however, he possess no control over the image produced from his flesh.

Oh, we are fearfully and wonderfully made: in the image of God; we are MAN.

God loved man before the foundation of the Earth, for we were in His spirit long before He created us. We were thought of, endeared, precious, and tender in his sight long before the foundation stone was set firmly in place on this planet. Long before the stars brightened

A Man Like God

the Heavens with their glory, the Lord embraced man in His heart.

THE CREATION

"And God said, Let us make man in our image, after our likeness: and let them have dominion over the fish of the sea, and over the fowl of the air, and over the cattle, and over all the earth, and over every creeping thing that creepeth upon the earth."

Genesis 1:26

What I like about God our Father is that He spoke everything into existence which He created: the stars; the sun and moon, plants, but He formed you and me in the person of the first man, Adam.

What this means is that God Himself reached down His mighty hands and shaped our bodies, molded our faces and sculpted our features with his bare hands.

It reveals that the man was a labor of love; a living, breathing piece of art by God Himself.

"So God created man in his own image, in the image of God created he him."

~Genesis 1:27

Man is not a haphazardly, evolved creature from a single-celled organism, but a perfect, sound, astute creation of the only wise God.

God stepped into the definite measurements of time, and shaped man from the dust of the ground, making sure every joint, bone, sinew, muscle, and flesh was perfectly shaped and covered in skin. Then finally, He coughed up a piece of his own spirit and breathed it into

THE MAN: CREATED

the nostril of the image he created, and man became a living SOUL.

Fundamentally then, man is not flesh but spirit. God breathed into the clay image of Himself and proclaimed it a living soul.

A soul is spirit and it is the spirit of man God always desired to commune with upon the earth.

God and God alone could then make this bold statement:

"Behold, all souls are mine; as the soul of the father, so also the soul of the son is mine: the soul that sinneth, it shall die."

~Ezekiel 18:4

Signs of Life

What a sight that must have been, to see Man take his first breath. To watch as the breath of God filled with the spirit of God and man enter into the form's nostrils. To witness his body transform from dust to flesh as the spirit of God moved throughout his body. The eyes fill in with color, the hair growing on his head and to see the beard break through the newly formed skin of his face. His ears take shape and the first sign of breath being inhaled as his chest rose and fell with a rhythmic rumble.

The first sound of his lungs inflating with air, the deafening sound of his first heartbeat and every move made representing the life of God has come to Earth. God, the Father, watching as a protective parent, as the man whom He created takes his first steps.

A Man Like God

Man, made in the image of God created as God on Earth, and having dominion over all creation, whom God named Adam; has now arrived. Everything is under his domain, his authority, his control; he is God on Earth, the man: **Adam**.

Have Dominion

"...and let them have dominion over the fish of the sea, and over the fowl of the air, and over the cattle, and over all the earth, and over every creeping thing that creepeth upon the earth."

~Genesis 1:26

Man was created to possess the same authority, power, and control over the earth as God has over his Heaven. God did not create man to be subservient to the earth, but the earth would serve man. In his created state Man is God in the Earth. Everything is under his domain and control. A stone is not moved without his word.

Since God the Father is King in Heaven, he has created man as King in the Earth. God the Father has made it illegal for even Him being spirit, to move a stone without the cooperation of Man. In this Law of Worlds and Realms, a disembodied spirit is given no authority in the Earth; unless given so by man.

However, by reason of the fact that Earth is in God's Realm; God the Father maintains authority over the Earth and man; God having created them.

KINGDOM ORDER

God works by Kingdom Rule, meaning everything operates by kingdom authority. Heaven then is the

THE MAN: CREATED

Kingdom of God. Earth is a territory of Heaven, namely The Kingdom of Heaven, which God placed Man to rule. Therefore, Man rules only by the will of God that will not be altered unless man disobeys God.

Kingdoms are transferred when a King dies or is overthrown either by force, pledge or (in the case of the Earth) deception. The same laws which govern Heaven also govern Earth. The difference here is Heaven has the knowledge of Good and Evil; the Earth at this time does not.

Therefore, the Man was created with no knowledge of Good or Evil, only peace and love. Man's true nature which God created him in, is to exist with peace and love all the days of his life; never knowing the pain of death, heartache, headache, sickness, or separation from God, the Father.

Heaven on Earth is what God had in mind and set out to create this experience on Earth:

"And the LORD God planted a garden eastward in Eden; and there he put the man whom he had formed. And out of the ground made the LORD God to grow every tree that is pleasant to the sight, and good for food; the tree of life also in the midst of the garden, and the tree of knowledge of good and evil. And a river went out of Eden to water the garden; and from thence it was parted, and became into four heads."

~Genesis 2:8-10

This kingdom created by God is to be governed in the same manner in which Heaven is governed; by sovereign rule. Meaning Adam (as well as all men) is to be King in the Earth, and everything created is to be subject to him. Adam is second only to God.

A Man Like God

Two kings cannot rule in the same kingdom or domain, therefore, God in wanting a creature like Himself needed him also to possess his own kingdom. Therefore, Earth was established as the domain of Man.

The laws or commandments of this kingdom were passed to the king Adam, and it is his duty to make sure all the creatures in his dominion obeyed and observed them.

The Commandment

"And the LORD God commanded the man, saying, Of every tree of the garden thou mayest freely eat: But of the tree of the knowledge of good and evil, thou shalt not eat of it: for in the day that thou eatest thereof thou shalt surely die."

~Genesis 2:16:17

What manner of place is this which only needed one commandment or law to govern its people?

Eden is a place where no time is kept; though time obviously exists time is not marked. Therefore, we do not know how long Man was in the garden alone before woman was created, whatever length of time it was, man lived without the knowledge of Good and Evil.

The Benefits

Adam is charged with naming all the animals of the earth:

"And out of the ground the LORD God formed every beast of the field, and every fowl of the air; and brought them unto Adam to see what he would call them: and whatsoever Adam called every living creature, that was the name thereof."

~Genesis 2:18

THE MAN: CREATED

Today it is an honor to have even one animal named after you, however, who could've imagine having the opportunity to name every living animal on the planet? How long would it take? How much time did he spend naming each and every mammal, invertebrates, and all types of creeping things creeping upon the face of the Earth?

God charged Adam with the keeping of the commandment, and with the power to enforce them. Therefore, when he neglected to enforce the commandment where Eve was concerned he was justly reprimanded. This clearly illustrated by the following scripture:

"...For unto whomsoever much is given, of him shall be much required: and to whom men have committed much, of him they will ask the more."

~Luke 12:48

God gave Adam the keys to the Kingdom of Heaven, with all the power, authority, and dominion to occupy the earth. He had the charge; he received the commandment, and he alone is responsible for the adherence of and to the law.

With all which men go through to be in authority or obtain power, Adam has power and authority thrust upon him simply because he is the son of God. He doesn't need to deceive, belittle, or manipulate anyone in order to obtain this power and authority. He only had to be who he was created to be.

A Man Like God

CREATED MAN

Here is a man perfect in his creation, peaceful, loving, strong, worshipper of God, sinless, having an intimate relationship with God, obedient, honest, trustworthy, man of his word, and holy.

Here is the man God created. In the image of God created He him (the man). Man, the spitting image of God having the authority, nature, and power of God on the earth and living in the peace of God. Everything man did prospered, because he has prosperity within him.

He is God in the flesh; that which is not he has the power to create. He reflects the glory of God in the Earth, and the earth loves him and bends to his will.

He does not know his limitations because there are no limitations. Whatever he can conceive he can receive. He calls those things which are not as though they were.

What lessons did God teach him? What an experience to walk with God in the cool of the day.

All we die to be he is; a **MAN** like God.

Chapter 2

THE MAN: HIS WO-MAN

Unique as man is, God yet looked upon him and said:

"It is not good for man to be alone; I will make a help meet for him."

~Genesis 1:28 with emphasis added

The scripture goes on to say out of the ground God formed every living creature of the earth, and brought them to Adam to witness what he would call them. Whatever Adam named them, was what they would be called forever. However, out of these were none found for Adam to be a help meet for him.

Therefore, the Lord God caused a deep sleep to fall upon Adam and from his side God removed a rib and created Adam a help meet (wife), whom Adam called Woman.

EVE

"And Adam said, This is now bone of my bones, and flesh of my flesh: she shall be called Woman, because she was taken out of Man."

~Genesis 2:23

When one considers the creation of a thing and desires to understand its purpose, one should go back to the original design, and compare to ascertain if its use is in conjunction with its original purpose. We can then

A Man Like God

understand where we went wrong and correct the error to begin using it was intended.

Such would be the case with the woman; we have gone so far off the mark of the intended purpose of a woman. She is not created to be our plaything, baby factory, or a place simply to relieve our sexual frustrations.

God created woman because He espied a void in the man that no other creature created filled. The fact that she was created with man's rib and not formed from the dust of the earth; signifies her status as his equal. Man should be able to gaze upon his wife and see himself as Adam gazed upon Eve and saw himself.

Adam knew in an instant he could never hurt her, demean her, mistreat her, or curse her without doing the same thing to himself. God beheld the two of them not as separate beings but one person, as if to say: you are not complete without her, and she is not complete without you; for she came from you. Therefore, she (your wife) is you even as we as men are God (if we accept Jesus as our personal savior), for we are one with God.

God breathed himself into the man, making man from himself and God formed woman from man, making the woman of the man.

Therefore, woman's name was called Eve giving her a place of honor next to her husband, signifying her status as Lord with her husband. At this time, she was not subordinate to her husband but ruled with him side by side as one.

THE MAN: HIS WO-MAN

The Softer Side of Man

God created Eve out of a rib taken from Adam's side rather than forming her fresh from the ground. Eve then was not made of the substance that Adam was made. She has been taken from Adam's support system, the part which protected his vital organs, which provided support for his frame. She' is made of that which is strong, firm, buoyant and flesh. Therefore, she is softer in nature, but strong in presence, to support her husband when he is weak.

THE UNBREAKABLE COVENANT

"Therefore shall a man leave his father and his mother, and shall cleave unto his wife: and they shall be one flesh."
~Genesis 2:24

God made an unbreakable covenant between created man and his wife which cannot neither be made with a written contract nor dissolved with a contract. This covenant is made with flesh and bone, its signature is created in man's DNA and is only canceled, or dissolved by the death of either party.

God took one rib from Adam and created one woman; Eve. Therefore, man is to possess one wife all his days, or until his wife dies as stated in scripture:

"The wife is bound by the law as long as her husband liveth; but if her husband be dead, she is at liberty to be married to whom she will; ***only in the Lord.***"

~1 Corinthian 7:39

In the Garden of Eden, no wedding celebration took place, no courtship (as far as we know) took place, and

A Man Like God

no sexual intercourse (again as far as we know) took place. Once Adam took knowledge that Eve was bone of his bone, and flesh of his flesh Eve became Adam's wife.

Adam's own DNA spoke out and perceived Eve was his and none other.

Okay, one could suggest they were the only two people in the Garden at the time and who else was Adam going to marry? However, I considered this would be too simplistic for a God, who is unsearchable.

Considering Adam was as God, he would understand Eve was a product of himself through God. Consider again, Adam had searched through all the creatures created and didn't find any among them to be a helpmeet for him. One look upon Eve and he recognized his own flesh? Wow, that's powerful.

Therefore, by reason of this the covenant of marriage to one woman has been established and confirmed by this word:

"Therefore shall a man leave his father and his mother, and shall cleave unto his wife: and they shall be one flesh."

~Genesis 2:24

MARRIAGE

"Husbands, love your wives, even as Christ also loved the church, and gave himself for it." Ephesians 5:25

First I must say marriage is not the way to escape from being single, or to avoid having sex out of wedlock. Marriage should not be entered into lightly,

THE MAN: HIS WO-MAN

or even to suggest one is living a life they truly are not living.

Marriage should not be entered into simply because one is lustful and can't control their sexual desires. If a man desires to be married because he cannot contain his desire as scripture teaches:

"But if they cannot contain, let them marry: for it is better to marry than to burn."

~1 Corinthians 7:9

Then he should understand, the marriage covenant is for life. Once you've made this covenant through your lust and find your lust has been fulfilled, and, therefore, you no longer want to be married, there is no escape clause written into this covenant. It is most certainly in the eyes of God unbreakable.

Though it may seem you make this covenant through a man-made system of licensing, this covenant is established by God in your flesh and not by letter from your state. Therefore, you enter this covenant or vow between you, your wife, and God. And God is not a covenant breaker.

Also, consider as written: *"Better is it that thou shouldest not vow, than that thou shouldest vow and not pay." Ecclesiastes 5:5 Again: "For the LORD, the God of Israel, saith that he hateth putting away (divorce)."*

~Malachi 2:16 with emphasis added

A Man Like God

Sexual Immorality of Men and Absent Fathers

We as men often go into marriage with the desire to be committed to one woman, but revel in our weakness to fall and commit adultery with other women. Of course, this is not the case with all men, but for the vast majority it is our manhood that makes us cheat (or at least this is our excuse), and a man who does not cheat runs the risk of being considered gay or weak.

We like children have made one particular excuse for far too long; "We are men, this is the reason we have or need lots of sex, or must be with different partners before we get married."

We've been taught by our parents (some women as well), not to settle down too soon. Bed as many women as you can before you get married; sow your wild oats, you know be a **Man**.

What we've ended up with are fatherless children, male children who don't know who they are, and don't understand how to respond in a loving, caring manner with their female counterparts. Devilish men, who mistreat and demean women, rather than nurture and preserve them as God intended men to do.

We've got female children who possess no knowledge of how to respond to a man, because they never received the love of their father; simply because many fathers became selfish in their insatiable pursuit of female flesh. Therefore, how can they teach daughters to cherish what they are ravishing on every corner?

What our daughters experience, are young boys and, unfortunately, men who only want to cherish what's

THE MAN: HIS WO-MAN

between their legs, and if they are not offering sex, we make them female dogs, whores and the like only in an attempt to make them feel less than who they are. Only so they will give up what they did not want to give in the first place.

Now in order to find a man, any man, women advertise their flesh with almost nothing on. She exposes her breasts to the point that only the nipple is not seen and this is what we men call sexy. Meanwhile, the men they are seeking are only coming to sex them and leave them with more fatherless children.

Congratulations, this is what we as men and fathers created because we've left the covenant of marriage, and have suffered ourselves to engage in sexual escapades rather than loving, nurturing relationships with our wives. We men taught our young men this. Not by what we say, but by what we've done. Children learn by example.

Many men are running out of ribs because you've married several women and have kept none of them.

Marriage happens when a man and a woman come together sexually, and his seed (sperm) passes from him to her. This act in God's eyes seals and confirms the bond of marriage.

Men, by misusing sex you have sealed many women to you by a blood covenant. The child born from this union is the witness and the agreement that you've broken covenant with those women to support them, nourish them, and keep them.

Therefore, the sin we've committed against God and women are great because we've given into lust, and

A Man Like God

married many women and left them destitute. Many men never or refuse to acknowledge the token of those unions represented by the children born through those encounters.

These are spiritual laws that govern marriage between a man and a woman. Marriage is not only a natural union, but a spiritual union, as well. Therefore, we need to repent before God and turn from our ungodly ways of giving into our lust, and allow God to deliver us before it is too late.

Husband's Role in Marriage

A husband is a man who is faithful in all his ways, and considers his mates feelings before his own, as is written:

"But he that is married careth for the things that are of the world, how he may please his wife."

~1 Corinthians 7:33

It is the husband's duty to put his wife's needs before his own, to make sure she possesses everything needed before he exits his home to take care of others. Conversely, the wife is to make sure her husband's needs are met before her own. In this manner, each is looking after the other and neither is neglected because they are not looking after themselves.

The husband is to love his wife as Christ loved the church and gave Himself for it (see Ephesians 5:25). Not being bitter toward the wife (see Colossians 3:19) but nourishing her as Christ does the Church.

THE MAN: HIS WO-MAN

For an example of this, we must consider how the Lord takes care of his church:

He often overlooks our faults and sees our needs. He is merciful to our sins, and when we repent He throws them into the sea of forgetfulness not holding them over our head. He laid down His own life for us his Church and He showers us with His tender mercies, and does not keep anger forever.

He became a curse for His church in order to redeem us unto Himself (see Galatians 3:13). The time would fail to name all the things which Christ did, and does for His church which He expects husbands to do for their wives.

No Divorce Clause

"But I say unto you, That whosoever shall put away his wife, saving (except) for the cause of fornication, causeth her to commit adultery: and whosoever shall marry her that is divorced committeth adultery."
~Matthew 5:32 with emphasis added

There is no excuse for husbands to put away their wives except for adultery (your wife's not yours).

What is the excuse you will give God in putting away your wife other than she had sex with another man? I do not love her anymore? She is not a wife to me because she does not give me sex when I want it? She is mean to me and won't let me hang with the boys. We've grown apart. We argue all the time. I can't do this anymore. Oh and I love this one: Irreconcilable Differences; which to this author means "there's no good excuse at all."

A Man Like God

None of these are excuses God will accept, and even though the church has embraced divorce; God has **NOT**!

When God took Adam's rib and made Eve He did not put a divorce clause in the rib after he created her. Adam knew and understood this woman was his responsibility for the balance of his life, which at the time had the potential to be eternity.

"For the LORD, the God of Israel, saith that he hateth putting away (divorce)."

~Malachi 2:16 with emphasis added

Now though Israel had been putting away their wives for centuries, God now through his servant Malachi lets Israel know he hated divorce. Who knew?

We often make our own laws, rules, and traditions to benefit ourselves, which God does not delight in nor approve.

The Pharisees asked Jesus this very question to which Jesus answered:

"He saith unto them, Moses because of the hardness of your hearts suffered you to put away your wives: but from the beginning it was not so."

~Matthew 19:8

Don't allow your heart to harden against the commandment of God. If you've divorced asked the Lord for forgiveness, and never marry again with divorce as an option.

If you suspect your marriage will not last forever, don't marry, and if you feel as if you can't maintain

The Man: His Wo-Man

your marriage until the end of your life…Pray for restoration.

One Exception

The only reason God has given for men to put away their wives with a bill of divorcement is adultery (sex with anyone other than your spouse). Sexual unfaithfulness in the heart of marriage is one of the most grievous acts a mate can do against their spouse.

Therefore, it is this act to which a man may divorce his wife and marry another. However, the woman he marries must be in the Lord; Saved and filled with the Holy Ghost. The divorced man or woman due to unfaithfulness must not be unequally yoked together with an unbeliever (see 2 Corinthians 6:14).

Wherefore, if the party that has been cheated on can forgive the spouse and release them from the betrayal, then they should forgive them and strengthen the marriage vow rather than separating.

Remember the many times God has forgiven you for your unfaithfulness to him. How dare you not forgive your spouse for her infidelity? When God has and continues to forgive you.

However, when both of you have been unfaithful to the marriage, you must choose to forgive one another, and not engage in adultery again. You've both been unfaithful to each other you are equally guilty. You shall not divorce, but work out your issues repenting to the Lord.

"Now, therefore, there is utterly a fault among you, because ye go to law one with another. Why do ye not rather

take wrong? why do ye not rather suffer yourselves to be defrauded?"

~1 Corinthians 6:7

It is important men learn to be faithful in all they do and say. As representatives of God in the Earth we, above all, must show an example of faithfulness as we are the head, and the true order of the family is: God - Husband–Wife– Children.

If a man be proven to be unfaithful who can trust him with anything, especially his own:

"And if ye have not been faithful in that which is another man's, who shall give you that which is your own?"

~Luke 16:12

If you cannot be trusted with something belonging to someone else, how will it be known that, that which you say is yours is yours?

Even scripture doubts whether a man in of himself can be faithful:

"Most men will proclaim everyone his own goodness: but a faithful man who can find?"

~Proverbs 20:6

Therefore, be found faithful in all you do, and do not commit to marriage if divorce is an option.

THE MARRIAGE BED DEFILED

"Marriage is honourable in all, and the bed undefiled: but whoremongers and adulterers God will judge."
~Hebrews 13:4

THE MAN: HIS WO-MAN

Most people believe the above scripture and take it to heart, so they do and allow anything to go on in the marriage bed because they've taken this scripture too far.

It is possible to defile the marriage bed, and I believe after you read the explanation given to me by the Lord you will agree:

Anything used contrary to the way it was created to be used or intended is in most cases abomination to the Lord. When a man upon his marriage bed takes his penis and enters the anus (sodomise) of his wife he commits abomination against God performing that which is against the natural use of the anus, and. Therefore, causes the marriage bed to be defiled.

Therefore, when a man desires to use his wife's body parts or functions for any other purpose than what it is meant to be used for, he defiles his marriage bed.

When a husband invites another partner, be it male or female and they engage in sexual intercourse together, they've defiled the marriage bed, because they have committed whoredom and adultery in their marriage. Also, they've invited the spirit of Homosexuality into the marriage (depending on the acts performed).

When that husband or wife goes out and has a sexual relationship with a partner of the same sex, they've defiled the marriage bed. Even though they did not do the act in the bed of union, they have yet defiled their sacred place because they took their committed bodies and have committed whoredom, abomination, and adultery with another person of the same sex.

A Man Like God

Remember the man and his wife are ONE person, not two, therefore, when either of them goes and has sexual intercourse or relationship with another man or woman, they force their mate to also have sex with said person. Therefore, if you've had sex with another female other than your wife, you have also caused your wife to engage in sex with the other woman, because you and your wife are not two different people, but the same person.

The Spirit of Lust

Lust is the enemy of any relationship or marriage. Causing division, separation, unfaithfulness, untruthfulness, envy, jealousy, pride, homosexuality, and the list goes on.

The spirit of lust works to make one concentrate on self, so all that is seen or desired is to make ones' self-feel good or satisfied. Lust is often confused with love because it gives one the overwhelming feeling of euphoria and is a catalyst for sexual immorality.

Men often confuse lust with the natural drive of a man to engage in sexual intercourse. However, when this desire is present and the man doesn't possess the ability to control himself it is no longer nature, but the spirit of lust.

Lust causes a man to masturbate, giving him self-pleasure continuously and omitting the use of the woman. Lust causes him to desire multiple mates apart from his wife. It' is also lust which is at the root of homosexuality causing the man to leave the natural use of the woman (see Romans 1:27).

The Man: His Wo-Man

Will you not be delivered from the spirit of lust which has blinded you, and given you a false sense of manhood? Will you not be free as a man of God, in the image of God who embraces the fruit of the enemy, simply because it makes your flesh feel good?

Will you justify your inability to keep your hands off the women in the congregation and make a mockery of God, under the false premise of manhood? Will you continue to bring the body of Christ to an open shame because of your inability to admit you have an issue with lust, and homosexuality that you may be free?

The Devil is laughing at us because we will not acknowledge our own frailties even to ourselves. Therefore, we hide in false marriages, false relationships, lying to ourselves, and content to continue lying to protect our own insecurities.

Wounding our women, casting down the image they have of themselves, because of our own inability to admit even to ourselves that we are less than we appear to be; puffed up by our own pride, so even the truth cannot bring us to the truth, and deliverance.

It is time that we be not men in nature, but men of God in God, by the spirit of God, and in the image of God MEN.

Only then can we TRULY embrace our WOMEN.

It is Good to be Virgins

"But I would have you without carefulness. He that is unmarried careth for the things that belong to the Lord, how he may please the Lord."

~1 Corinthians 7:32

A Man Like God

Paul states in scripture it is good for a man to remain unmarried. A cuss word to too many in the Body of Christ, because as with many of the scriptures we've taken this particular scripture too far:

"And the LORD God said, It is not good that the man should be alone; I will make him an help meet for him."

~Genesis 2:18

Just because God said it's not good for man to be alone, does not mean he shouldn't be alone, or he can't be alone. Both Jesus and Paul were great examples of men in the Bible who were not married, and lived perfect lives without being married. They also were not alone; Jesus and Paul had the Holy Ghost to keep them.

Man is not all together weak, or gay, or anything in between because he is not married, or engaged in sex with a woman. He should not be looked upon as strange because he is 38 and not married yet. It is wise for a man to remain unmarried when he feels he is not ready or mature enough to be faithful to the marriage covenant.

It is further wise, that he not to bow himself over a woman he has not committed himself to in marriage, simply to be counted as a man in the eyes of men.

Paul by the spirit of God wrote:

"A man who is unmarried cares for the things that belong to the Lord, how he may please the Lord."

~1 Corinthians 7:32

He understood when a man is unmarried he can devote his time, energy, and resources to following the Lord's will completely.

THE MAN: HIS WO-MAN

This author have found it much easier to go and come doing the Lord's will without being encumbered with the duties of a husband; knowing well the duties of a husband could impede greatly on the ability to perform freely my duties with the Lord. That is impede not stop.

Singleness then is the will of God, however, not in the manner in which we count singleness.

Being single is about being one with the Father, the Son, and the Holy Ghost. It means to possess one-mind, one-purpose, and one focus; one in mind, body, and spirit.

When one is truly single, he is not encumbered with past issues, problem, or relationships. Someone claiming to be single and yet harbors feelings for a past relationship, or is pining over a past relationship; is not single.

Therefore, being single does not mean one is absent of a committed relationship or dating someone.

Many of us do not even possess a single relationship with the Lord, because we are encumbered with so many other things in our life that we have to schedule the Lord in, instead of everything else being scheduled around the Lord.

Singleness is about being unified with the Spirit of God. You and He becomes one in mind, body, and spirit.

A virgin should be; single in mind, body, and spirit as well as never having been with someone sexually.

A Man Like God

Once you are divided in thought it will not be long before you are also divided in body and spirit.

MARRY A VIRGIN

"There is difference also between a wife and a virgin. The unmarried woman careth for the things of the Lord, that she may be holy both in body and in spirit: but she that is married careth for the things of the world, how she may please her husband."

~1 Corinthians 7:34

Our very own Apostle Paul was a virgin having never touched a woman. Selah

It was not lawful for a man as an Israelite to touch a woman before they were married and, therefore, the men and women remained virgins until the day they came together in the wedding chamber. Paul obeyed the law and lived under the strictest sect of the Pharisees until the day of his conversion, and remained unmarried after his conversion and, therefore, a virgin until the day of his death.

It is the will of God that all men and woman remain virgins until the day they are married.

It was even unlawful for the priest to marry any woman unable to prove their virginity. The priest was not allowed to marry a widow:

"And he (the priest) shall take a wife in her virginity. A widow, or a divorced woman, or profane, or an harlot, these shall he not take: but he shall take a virgin of his own people to wife."

~Leviticus 21:13-14 with emphasis added

The Man: His Wo-Man

We are kings and priests of God (see 1 Peter 2:9), and, therefore, should not (help me Lord Jesus) be marrying women who are not virgins. In reality, as children of the Most High God, there should not be a woman or man among us who's never been married that is not a virgin.

However, it is understood, that many of us who came out of sin have engaged in sex out of wedlock (fornication) and, therefore, are not virgins.

The Lord can make women who came out of sin virgins again by spirit for old things become new (see 2 Corinthians 5:17).

These must after their conversions not engage in sex with a man until they are married, thus honoring themselves, God, and their future husbands with their clean bodies.

Therefore, a woman who's been born-again to Christ may be engaged to marry and considered a virgin in Christ; only if she has not been with a man after her conversion. The same is true with a man.

Wherefore, their old sin has been washed away by the blood of Jesus Christ, and they are a new creation in Christ Jesus. They should not, however, be married right after their conversion, but should remain single for a time until they are single in mind, body, and spirit; representing their separation of purity.

Now let me be very clear on what the Lord is saying: We should be virgins until married, and only marry women who are virgins never having had sex with a man; or converted women who have never been with a man after their conversion.

A Man Like God

If a woman who's engaging in sex after her conversion repents, and remains untouched by a man for a season, she may be considered for marriage. However, if she turns and again begins to miss-use her temple with men or women she should remain unmarried and faithful to God, though she would be forgiven if she repents.

Reestablishing the Sanctity of Virginity

In order to reestablish the virginity of men and women in the Body of Christ we as men must embrace this teaching of scripture, and our Lord and savior Jesus Christ.

We must put aside our own improper dealings with sex and be delivered of lust and all sexual immorality of the flesh. We as leaders must teach our young men and women to honor their bodies which are the temple of the Holy Ghost, and train them with strict distain in resisting sexual immorality.

We must further separate ourselves from the world and it's teachings of sexual freedom that is contrary to the teachings of our Lord and savior Jesus Christ. We must do this by example as well as teachings of scripture.

We must understand sexual intercourse is not natural if it is not used in a manner to which God commanded it to be utilized. Youth is not an excuse to disobey the Lord in engaging in sex out of the marriage covenant.

God is calling us back to cleanliness, and purity of spirit. That also includes our body, we must do as

THE MAN: HIS WO-MAN

scripture stated: "*I beseech you therefore, brethren, by the mercies of God, that ye present your bodies a living sacrifice, holy, acceptable unto God, which is your reasonable service.*"

~Romans 12:1

Fathers do this by teaching their sons and daughters at home. We do this by not looking at our women with lust filled eyes, and encouraging them to honor their bodies. Not giving women the attention they want when they dress in inappropriate clothing, but demanding they dress and carry themselves as women professing holiness and godliness (see 1 Timothy 2:9-10).

Men, we are the catalyst for clean living in the Body of Christ. Women dress the way they think we want them to dress, in order to gain our attention, and we in our own lust caused them to err in this manner. We must then begin to turn the tides so we may once again bring true honor to our women.

Break covenant with me that we will never again bring our women to such a state in which they feel the need even in the Body of Christ to present themselves half dressed, or with their breast exposed.

Stand with me in holding ourselves responsible for the many children who walk into our services without fathers. Let us hold our men responsible who father children and refuse to take care of them.

If there are men in our midst who have fathered children and are not paying child support, we should refuse to congregate with them, or better yet encourage them to begin to take responsibility for the children they fathered. Should they be unable to take care of

A Man Like God

their children, let the true church help in supporting his children until he can do so himself (making sure to give him the tools to take care of his own children).

Make sure they obtain DNA testing to verify they fathered these children, and cause them to take responsibility of the children as well as the women with whom they fathered children.

It is written: *"But if any provide not for his own, and specially for those of his own house, he hath denied the faith, and is worse than an infidel (one who has no faith)."*

~1Timothy 5:8

How many infidels have you allowed to play in your presence?

The word "house" in the scripture above is not speaking of house as in building, or structure, but lineage as in family or offspring. Therefore, to allow our young people to come into our midst, especially our young women with children and not cause the men (boys) to meet this responsibility; we are participating in their sins.

We've been lapse for far too long in allowing this behavior to continue. If they leave, then let them leave, but we must bring back the sanctity of virginity to our young men and women. The spirit of the Lord demands it of us. Our women crave it of us. We as men need it. How many of us need to die before we wake up and take note; we must go back to the Bible way of doing things?

Come on Men. Gird up the loins of your mind and let's embrace the truth of who we are, and who we are

The Man: His Wo-Man

to be to our women. Don't you think we have let them down for far too long?

"All the ways of a man are clean in his own eyes; but the LORD weigheth the spirits."

~Proverbs 16:2

"Remember therefore from whence thou art fallen, and repent, and do the first works; or else I will come unto thee quickly, and will remove thy candlestick out of his place, except thou repent."

~Revelation 2:5

Chapter 3

THE MAN: FALLEN

Too often, it seems as though as things begin to go well we always find a way to mess our life up. Be it our insecurities or our desire to be in the "in crowd," we always seem to cause our own demise.

Through our decisions, we cause things to work in our favor or work against us. What is the issue with men that cause us to hinder what was for our benefit to turn around for our harm?

While many of us would blame someone else for our demise, the truth is; it is often our own decisions which cause our difficulties.

Now after so many thousands, or millions of years of being in the Garden with his wife, having no issues at all; here comes some old fool who doesn't like the fact of anyone doing well, or having a good time.

"Now the serpent was more subtil than any beast of the field which the LORD God had made. And he said unto the woman, Yea, hath God said, Ye shall not eat of every tree of the garden?"

~Genesis 3:1

No doubt Eve had spoken to this particular serpent many times before with no issue, but on this day unbeknownst to Eve; Satan had entered the serpent and began to tempt her with what God had commanded.

A Man Like God

Therefore, we catch Eve speaking with the serpent ignorant of the fact that a trap has been set for her and Adam's demise.

Their conversation continues: *"And the woman said unto the serpent, We may eat of the fruit of the trees of the garden: But of the fruit of the tree which is in the midst of the garden, God hath said, Ye shall not eat of it, neither shall ye touch it, lest ye die."*

~Genesis 3:2-3

Eve understood well the commandment of God, understanding death, being separation from God, would occur if she and Adam ate the forbidden fruit: but, Satan in his craftiness tempted Eve with the very thing we all desire to achieve; to be like God.

"And the serpent said unto the woman, Ye shall not surely die: For God doth know that in the day ye eat thereof, then your eyes shall be opened, and ye shall be as gods, knowing good and evil."

~Genesis 3:4-5

A twist of words trapped Eve in lust, and she began to desire the forbidden fruit to which God had said: *"You shall not eat of the tree of Knowledge of Good and Evil."*

You know the rest of the story; Eve ate of the forbidden fruit and also gave to her husband Adam, who also ate the forbidden fruit. Now it is not until Adam ate the fruit that their eyes became opened, and they knew they were naked and became ashamed.

THE MAN: FALLEN

SIN AND DEATH INTERRUPTS PARADISE

"And unto Adam he said, Because thou hast hearkened unto the voice of thy wife, and hast eaten of the tree, of which I commanded thee, saying, Thou shalt not eat of it: cursed is the ground for thy sake; in sorrow shalt thou eat of it all the days of thy life; Thorns also and thistles shall it bring forth to thee; and thou shalt eat the herb of the field; In the sweat of thy face shalt thou eat bread, till thou return unto the ground; for out of it wast thou taken: for dust thou art, and unto dust shalt thou return."

~Genesis 3:17-19

Here we go with lust again. Eve determined that the tree was good for food, and was pleasant to the eyes, and a tree to be desired to make one wise (see Genesis 3:6). According to the scriptures:

"Then when lust hath conceived, it bringeth forth sin: and sin, when it is finished, bringeth forth death."

~James 1:15

The lust of Eve's eyes brought her to sin against the commandment of God, which by the disobedience of Adam; brought death upon all.

Understand, Adam and Eve is one Man. Therefore, sin was not complete until Adam also ate of the forbidden fruit making sin complete in man. Adam could have chosen not to eat of the forbidden fruit making Eve's transgression null and void.

On the contrary, Adam chose to sacrifice himself for Eve in order to save her alive. He in this action became the picture of Jesus Christ, who also came to sacrifice

A Man Like God

himself to redeem us from our sinful nature back to God.

Therefore, Adam, a man who has been created the head, is responsible for the death of all things coming on the Earth, and not Eve alone: for in Adam all die (see 1 Corinthians 15:22).

Here now is the birth of sin in the Earth. Eden becomes the birthplace of death in man; both spiritual and natural. Adam is punished with physical death; for God cursed Adam saying:

"In the sweat of thy face shalt thou eat bread, till thou return unto the ground; for out of it wast thou taken: for dust thou art, and unto dust shalt thou return."

~Genesis 3:19

Therefore, because man includes woman all flesh dies. Not only does this death affect man, but death also affects every living thing on the planet.

Adam is the godhead in the earth and, therefore, is held responsible for the sin of the world. Disobedience caused men to be held responsible for all the discord shed from Adam to Jesus. Therefore, there are two types of men on Earth; those who still live under the curse of Adam, and those who are redeemed by the sacrifice of Jesus Christ.

THE KINGDOM STOLEN

"Nevertheless death reigned from Adam to Moses, even over them that had not sinned after the similitude of Adam's transgression, who is the figure of him that was to come."
~Romans 5:14

THE MAN: FALLEN

God established the Kingdom on Earth by His righteousness, having created man in His image and nature, and ordained the man to possess dominion over the kingdoms on Earth, but man forfeited his dominion when he sinned against God.

The kingdom then transferred to Satan, who has now cast his nature upon man (Satan's nature being sinful: any act of a person against the nature or commandment of God).

By the single act of Adam's disobedience to God, he's cast down the nature of God in himself and taken on the nature of Satan. Whose desire is to ascend above the heights of the clouds, and be like the most High (see Isaiah 14:14). The problem here is he (Satan) can only create death not life. Thus, death has entered the world.

Therefore, being the Kingdom is established by righteousness, and man has now taken on the nature of Satan, God chases Adam out of the Garden of Eden lest he should take hold of the Tree of Life and live forever in sin (Genesis 3:24).

Man is now as it were on his own in the world, to work, live, and die by the sweat of his brow. This is the curse of Adam (Adamic Curse); this is the curse men fall under when we do not accept the sacrifice of Jesus on the cross.

By a decision of one-man death, hell, and the grave has been prescribed upon all flesh. Having been made in the image of God, we now take on the nature of Satan and begun to fill our hearts with the fruits of the Devil.

Which include: murder, the lie, hypocrisy, fornication (premarital sex), pride, lust, envy, jealousy,

A Man Like God

hatred (the same is murder), anger, homosexuality, whoredom, prostitution, sodomy, molestation, rape, and all sin which the Lord hates.

The Kingdom of Earth is now soiled with the sin of Satan, and man's heart becoming extremely wicked, God now repents (grieves or changes his mind) Himself for even creating man (see Genesis 6:6). However, because of His mercy he devises a plan to keep men alive upon the earth, and redeem him to Himself again.

The Glory has Departed

God having removed himself far from man, the Glory of God departs from the earth. Left are sin, destruction, and death. Glorying of flesh has taken over; for men became lovers of revelry, sex, murder, hating one another, and abusing themselves with the daughters of men, and mankind.

God's heart smote within Him because man had fallen into sin. His heritage has become a den for all manner of sin and shame. Therefore, he thought to destroy man off the face of the earth (see Genesis 6:13).

Thanks to one-faithful man God found a way to keep men alive upon the earth, and not to destroy him altogether.

Noah was found faithful in his entire house to the God of Heaven, and God chose him and his sons to keep men alive upon the earth.

Noah made an ark by the commandment of God and saved seven of every clean beast and creeping things, and two of the unclean beast and creeping things; the

THE MAN: FALLEN

male and his female including Noah and his family to preserve life upon the earth.

But men grew worse and worse, however, God gave a promise to Noah,

"...I will not again curse the ground any more for man's sake; for the imagination of man's heart is evil from his youth; neither will I again smite any more everything living, as I have done?"

~Genesis 8:21

The old Earth having been done away with taking the curse of the ground against men away with it, God now promises he will never again curse the ground for man's sake. For the imagination of man's heart, said God is evil from his youth.

However, the curse of death and the curse upon Eve God did not remove. We can still see the curse of death, and the curse upon Eve today, as people are still dying, and women are still bearing children in pain and suffering, as well as is required being in subjection, or subordinate to their own husbands (see Ephesians 5:22).

It is important to note here that a man is not evil from the womb but from his youth (see Genesis 8:21), when the child begins to have reasoning skills and can choose between the good and evil. However, we were yet conceived in sin (the curse of Adam) and shaped in iniquity (see Psalm 51:5). Therefore, we have the signature of sin already mapped in our flesh.

Demons attach themselves to babies after they are born growing with that child into adulthood. Herein lays the reason a gay male can say I always knew I was

A Man Like God

gay, because the spirit of homosexuality attached itself to him from a babe.

It therefore, becomes very difficult for him to resist this spirit because it is familiar to him. Natural if you will. He neither understands nor acknowledges that that which he prescribes to himself to be natural is not even him, but a demonic spirit. Such is the case with many of the sins that man does.

A heterosexual male may also be attacked at birth with the spirit of lust (we call this spirit a playa now), and lust stands as a gateway spirit to many other sins such as pride, arrogance, jealousy, promiscuity, hatred which is murder, witchcraft, horoscope, and many others.

Lust, pride, and arrogance are the three deadly sins to a man. It is the leading reason we have many women left with fatherless children and men who will not even bother to check paternity to see if they have fathered children.

Rather, some immediately deny they fathered a child, and place the blame upon the woman, instead of taking responsibility for their actions, and at least verify paternity. Making it possible, to stop this enclave of children who have no father, at least in the Body of Christ.

Our Adversary

"Be sober, be vigilant; because your adversary the devil, as a roaring lion, walketh about, seeking whom he may devour."
~1 Peter 5:8

THE MAN: FALLEN

The devil, Satan, Lucifer, Beelzebub, serpent, dragon are some of the names given to the devil. No matter what you call him he is our adversary. He is the accuser of the brethren (see Revelations 12:10), and is bent on our destruction no matter the cost. He hates you because you remind him of God being made in the image of God; so every time he encounters you, he encounters God. At least he should.

He's reminded every time he looks at you the reason he was kicked out of heaven:

"For thou hast said in thine heart, I will ascend into heaven, I will exalt my throne above the stars of God: I will sit also upon the mount of the congregation, in the sides of the north: I will ascend above the heights of the clouds; I will be like the most High."

~Isaiah 14:13-14

The devil's been kicked out of heaven because he lifted himself up in pride against God, being in close relationship with God. Here now God's created Man and made him only a little lower than Himself:

"What is man, that thou art mindful of him? and the son of man, that thou visitest him? For thou hast made him a little lower than the angels, and hast crowned him with glory and honor. Thou madest him to have dominion over the works of thy hands; thou hast put all things under his feet."

~Psalms 8: 4-6

The word translated angels in the KJV is actually Elohim in Hebrew and should be translated God. Therefore, God made man a little lower than Himself

A Man Like God

elevating man even above Satan and the angels of heaven: having breathed into man His own spirit.

You can see now why Satan is angry with man and he is going about depending on the ignorance of man to destroy himself.

"My people are destroyed for lack of knowledge."

~Hosea 4:6

Satan's greatest defense against man is that man doesn't know who he is and goes about establishing himself based on his five senses and emotions, rather than on his inheritance.

Our manhood is based mainly on what swings between our legs, the degrees we carry, the status and positions in life we hold, the beauty of our face or lack thereof, and the amount of money in our bank accounts; superficial things which we can neither take with us nor sell to extend our life.

The sad thing is the Devil doesn't need to do much to cause us to destroy ourselves. He makes a few suggestions and we run headlong, barely considering the outcome, or the danger to our souls. He has caused us to elevate our penis which in comparison, is a small member above everything else which makes us men.

If we consider what truly makes us men our penis would be far down the list, yet it's foremost on our minds only because of the pleasurable feeling we obtain when we have an orgasm.

Many of us would do just about anything to continue experiencing this same feeling of euphoria, as many times as possible no matter the consequences. And we

THE MAN: FALLEN

have, including risking eternal life for a moment of pleasure, and rejecting the Lord Jesus in order to continue our lustful ways.

Satan possesses such advantage over us knowing the Glory awaiting us on the other side, and doing his best to cause us never to obtain such glory, because of lust, pride, and arrogance.

Tools of The Adversary

"Lest Satan should get an advantage of us: for we are not ignorant of his devices."
~2 Corinthians 2:11

The tools the enemy uses to keep us in bondage are vast, but not insurmountable through Jesus Christ.

His tools include works of the flesh, religion, and demonic spirits who deceive and plant evil thoughts in our minds.

Works of the Flesh

"Now the works of the flesh are manifest which are these; Adultery, fornication, uncleanness, lasciviousness (Exciting sexual desires), Idolatry, witchcraft, hatred, variance (discrepancy or at odds with), emulations (An ambition and effort to equal, excel or surpass another), wrath, strife, seditions (conduct or language inciting rebellion against the authority of a state or God), heresies (any belief or theory that is strongly at odds with established beliefs or customs), Envyings, murders, drunkenness, reveling (noisy partying), and such like: of the which I tell you before, as I have also told you in time past, that they which do such things shall not inherit the kingdom of God."

A Man Like God

~Galatians 5:19-21 with emphasis added

The works of the flesh listed above in the scripture reference can be found, unfortunately, right in the Body of Christ. We've taken the things of the World to draw the World to our services, and, therefore, invited these evils back into our lives. Our services are now noisy parties rather than true praise and worship.

The only thing defining our music as gospel is subliminal words. The music is transformed to entice the world into our congregations, and Jesus is hardly the name recognized in the music we say represents Him.

In truth, we never gave up our sexual uncleanliness, because we view such as a natural part of our manhood. However, whatever is not used in the manner in which the Father intended does not represent God, but man and, therefore, the Devil.

Sex is not natural out of the marriage covenant. The exciting sexual desires we males take so much pride in is a work of the flesh and, therefore, a product of Satan, in a word; lust.

Therefore, because you are married does not mean lust is not present. In fact, if you engage in sex in a manner to which your body part was never intended, it becomes a product of lust, exciting sexual desires (lasciviousness), and defiles the marriage bed.

Satan is betting you will choose rather to enjoy the lust of your flesh, and the exciting sexual desires it craves. Rather than submit to the approved sexual intercourse which God created to be between a man and his wife.

THE MAN: FALLEN

To desire to witness two women engaging in sexual relations (which seems to be a fantasy for many men) is most definitely a product of lust. It is lasciviousness as well as homosexuality, and a product of Satan.

A man like God would not even allow himself to think such things that is conceived in the mind (lust is conceived in the mind). Thoughts conceived in the mind will get into the heart, and be expressed through the flesh as James says:

"*Then when lust hath conceived, it bringeth forth sin: and sin, when it is finished, bringeth forth death.*"

~James 1:15

All works of the flesh will cause you to miss your flight with Jesus when he returns, so gird up the loins of your mind and hope to the end that you will be able to escape the damnation of hell through Jesus Christ.

Religion

Religion is a collection of belief systems, cultural systems, and worldviews that relate humanity to spirituality and, sometimes, to moral values. Therefore, anything can be a religion representing any belief man holds which relate to some spiritual being or deity, and does not need to be based in truth.

Our adversary desires to keep us in religion which produces doctrines of devils, false security in a dead system which only proves to bind one to a system of man-made rules and traditions of men. Enslaving us to commandments of men and worshipping of the temporal rather than the eternal.

A Man Like God

Religion birthed the false teaching of Sinner Saved by Grace, which seeks to bind us to our sinful nature which Jesus died to free us from. Therefore, because we are Sinners Saved by Grace, the fact some constantly fall into sin is understandable even expected, excepted as regular human frailty rather than ungodly, unholy teachings of a demon bent on keeping us tethered to sin.

Yet, we buy into, purchase to ourselves these false teachings and will even use the Holy Scriptures to justify sin, when scripture does in no way justify sin or sinner.

This scripture is one of many which are used to justify continued sin:

"For all have sinned, and come short of the glory of God."

~Romans 3:23

In truth all have sinned, past tense and come short of the glory of God, however, thanks to the sacrifice of Jesus Christ on the cross, there's no need to continue in sin as revealed by scripture:

"What shall we say then? Shall we continue in sin, that grace may abound? God forbid. How shall we, that are dead to sin, live any longer therein?"

~Romans 6:1-2

Have you ever seen a dead man sin?

"Likewise reckon ye also yourselves to be dead indeed unto sin, but alive unto God through Jesus Christ our Lord."

~Romans 6:11

"For ye are dead, and your life is hid with Christ in God." Colossians 3:3 *"Therefore we are buried with him by baptism*

THE MAN: FALLEN

into death: that like as Christ was raised up from the dead by the glory of the Father, even so we also should walk in newness of life."

~Romans 6:4

If we, as some suppose, are yet sinners who are saved by grace, why did Jesus die to take away our sin; if He was going to leave us in sin, and save us over our sin anyway? Couldn't He save us without the formality of dying on the cross, becoming a curse for us that He may redeem us from sin? I speak as a fool.

Are we foolish enough to think God would send His only begotten son to die for the world to take away their sin, only to leave their sin intact and save them anyway? God, who can't be in the presence of sin, would send His Holy Spirit into a sin-filled life without first removing the sin?

The same God, who cannot sin, would accept our sin and save us anyway? Why do we repent of sin only to remain sinners saved by grace?

Religion, in other words, Satan, has blinded our eyes to accept an obviously false teaching and call it truth.

Rather than search the scripture to see if those things are so, we follow along because we've been deceived in thinking that blindly following religious leaders is the will of God.

Religion led us to believe falsehoods, and doctrines of devils to keep us in bondage to sin and, therefore, death.

"Now if we be dead with Christ, we believe that we shall also live with him."

A Man Like God

~Roman 6:8

The Lord Jesus is not into religious acts, but a genuine relationship with Him, which transforms the lives of those who come in contact with Him. However, Satan desires you to be engrossed in religious acts, worshipping of the building (temporal) more than truly worshipping God the Father by Jesus Christ (eternal).

Therefore, we have "church," rather than becoming the true temples of a Holy God.

"What? *Know ye not that your body is the temple of the Holy Ghost which is in you, which ye have of God, and ye are not your own?*"

~1 Corinthians 6:19

Your body is the "**House of God**," not a brick and mortar building to which you prescribed as the house of God. You are who God is trying to fill with his spirit, not a dead building. "*Howbeit the most High dwelleth not in temples made with hands…*" Acts 7:48

Though you build these great, beautiful swelling buildings and write upon them "The House of the Living God," God is not living there, but a living building made of flesh and blood he's chosen to put His name there:

"*Wherefore when he cometh into the world, he saith, Sacrifice and offering thou wouldest not, but a body hast thou prepared me.*"

~Hebrews 10:5

THE MAN: FALLEN

The Temporal Worship

God already tested the temporal worship in which He constructed a building for His spirit to rest in, a symbol of what was to come.

The tabernacle in the wilderness and the shedding of animal blood couldn't make the comers thereto perfect, who came every year to offer sacrifices and burnt offerings for sin, because them who came left continually with the remembrance of sin.

Therefore, God said: *"Sacrifice and offering thou didst not desire; mine ears hast thou opened: burnt offering and sin offering hast thou not required. Then said I, Lo, I come: in the volume of the book it is written of me, I delight to do thy will, O my God."*

~Psalms 40:6:8

In that the first tabernacle (church) did not prove to keep the comers thereunto perfect, or their conscious free of sin, the Lord prepared a body for Jesus to come and make an eternal sacrifice. A sinless body which Jesus used to condemn sin in the flesh giving us an example; that through Him we could live without sin in the flesh; for, without Him, we can do nothing (see John 15:5).

Therefore, we are inexcusable whichever of us attempt to justify our sinful ways before God, and attempt to say we can't do what Jesus did, simply because we are not Jesus. This is a lie the enemy would like you to believe, but Jesus told us we would do greater works than He did, and also scripture tells us:

A Man Like God

"Herein is our love made perfect, that we may have boldness in the Day of Judgment: because as he is, so are we in this world."

~1 John 4:17

As stated, Satan would love to keep us in the dark concerning who we are, in an attempt to keep us living beneath our true ability in Christ Jesus; to keep us in a perpetual fallen state and never able to see ourselves beyond our human limitations.

However, the only limitation to us in Christ Jesus is our faith:

"Jesus said unto him, If thou canst believe, all things are possible to him that believeth."

~Mark 9:23

Our adversary has done a great job in keeping us in a perpetual state of sin, keeping us in darkness to who we truly are in Christ.

Unable to grasp the fact that we are no longer born of sin, but of the righteousness of Jesus Christ in his blood; we who've accepted Jesus as our personal Lord and savior, and do not perform our own wills, but in spirit and truth worship the Father of spirits out of a pure heart.

Therefore, setting Jesus as our example we can walk in the newness of the spirit, and not in the letter; for the letter kills, but the spirit gives life (see 2 Corinthians 3:6).

We, therefore, who have accepted Jesus as Lord and savior are no longer under the curse of Adam, but in the freedom of Jesus Christ. Sin contains no more dominion

THE MAN: FALLEN

over us, and we, therefore do not need to obey lust in our flesh.

We are not ruled by sin and the lust that resides in our flesh, but we can choose to walk in the spirit so as not to fulfill the lust of the flesh (see Galatians 5:16).

"For the flesh lusteth against the Spirit, and the Spirit against the flesh: and these are contrary the one to the other: so that you cannot do the things that ye would."

~Galatians 5:17

Lust keeps you from doing the things your spirit desires to do, keeping you bound to a dead system, which in turn kills your spirit and keeps you in a vicious circle of sexual perversions, and lusting after things which are not convenient.

This is the goal of Satan to keep you in the flesh continuously, so you will not do the things you would in Christ.

Therefore, he keeps you in bondage to a physical building when God has shed his spirit within you, making you a living breathing temple, which cannot be limited by temporal worship.

Our minds have been geared to think of the building we worship in as the House of God, and our bodies become second-class citizens to the building. With God, you are important; you are "the church." You are the House of God, because God is alive and he requires a living house. Therefore, keep yourself clean and unspotted from the world.

A Man Like God

Man's Worship in God's View

You must understand how God views our worship: currently, the building is the central part of our worship. We make sure everything is neat and in order, everything has a place, and purpose. We make sure the brass is polished just so and dare anyone to touch them after they've been cleaned. We make sure no one plays in or around the sacred altar, and the pulpit is held in high regard.

Yet our bodies where resides the Holy Ghost we take and we lay-down with whomever, and whatever we please. We as men never verify the authenticity of the women we lay with, in order to satisfy our own desire; with the Holy Ghost right there and never considering perhaps the person we're laying with is also the Temple of the Living God (being filled with the Holy Ghost).

Our bodies are the temple of the Holy Ghost; the same spirit which resided in the Ark of the Covenant to which God slew a man for touching to steady it on a cart.

We take our bodies and allow any and everything to go on with not even a thought or conviction: the Holy Ghost lives inside of us. Making the physical building more important than the building where the Holy Ghost actually lives.

We write songs, and say prayers asking the Lord to fill our physical brick and mortar buildings, but not to fill his true temple; YOU.

THE MAN: FALLEN

We allow all manner of filth to cross our minds, when we would not dear to allow the bathroom in our worship centers to remain filthy for any length of time.

We worship the temporal and neglect the eternal. This is why we witness pastors, prophet, apostles, falling before the congregation because we've not honored the true temple of the Living God. We've not truly given honor where honor is due.

Men for the most part do not truly worship in the midst of the congregation; because of course, worship of God is a woman's job. We stand stiff as a board and watch, but God forbid many of us should even lift a hand in true worship. God forbid we should lose our composure for the cause of Christ and appear weak before the women in the so-called church.

It's required of God that men be found faithful even in worship because we are the carriers of the Image of God. David understood this and, therefore, had no problems losing himself in dancing out of his clothes in worship of his God.

Demonic Spirits

Satan does not work alone in attempting to draw men to his side, nor was he kicked out of heaven alone, but he took a third of the angels with him (see Revelations 12:4). These demons work under the authority of Satan to hinder, block, oppose, and destroy as many men as possible.

Demon spirits can plant thoughts in the mind, torment, condemn, persuade, possess, and oppress men into doing whatever they want. They possess the

A Man Like God

understanding and wisdom to use your emotions, five senses to get the response they desire to keep you bound in your emotions, and fleshly desires for as long as they please; or until you turn to the Lord.

They are relentless, and will not giveback easily, territory they've concurred without the spirit of the Lord forcing them to do so.

While you are vying for positions in a building demons are taking over territory in geographical regions. While you are competing for members for your building, demons are stealing souls for his kingdom; hell.

While the so called church is trying to bring sinners to 'church' demons are going where they are and sealing them in sin and death. All the while keeping us in a hypocritical state, compromising the Gospel of Jesus Christ; all in an attempt to keep the members we have because you know, we don't want to offend anyone.

Bringing us to an open shame, and making Holiness a joke because we thought our sins were being hid from the world; forcing God to expose great leaders, because we did not separate the profane from the holy, and went about establishing our own righteousness in our own eyes.

Demons deceive making possible for some to teach and package a false doctrine right under the nose of those who think they are most learned among us. Causing us to view gain as godliness, being greedy of filthy lucre, and calling it prosperity. However,

THE MAN: FALLEN

godliness with contentment is great gain (see 1Timothy 6:6).

Demons are in the midst of our worship, in our music; while we say we are dancing for the Lord, and in our learned behaviors of worship. Right there while we participate in communion and plotting our premeditated sins after we leave, having repented before we partake of communion, but can't wait to leave in order to fill up on sin again.

Demons right there while we laugh, joke, jest and poke fun at those who we deem least among us; swollen up with pride because our faults haven't been exposed yet. While we condemn those who've fallen from grace, and not taking note; it could've been us.

Quick to judge but slow to pray, demons are all around us. What have you given thim license to do in your life today?

ADAM WHERE ARE YOU?

This question is still being asked of many men today, because they have no clue who they are. Nor yet do they understand the extent of whose they are, or the vastness of what they possess the ability to accomplish through Jesus Christ.

Our faith is so low we are unable to fathom doing even the minute things the Lord commanded us to do; like be perfect. This small task is blown to high heavens because we view our inability to be perfect in our flesh, but neglect to understand that through the Spirit of the Lord, the commandments of God are fulfilled, and nothing is impossible.

A Man Like God

Not by power, nor by might, but by my spirit says the Lord (see Zechariah 4:6).

It is by the Spirit of the Lord man is obedient; it is not in him to be obedient on his own. It's by the Spirit of the Lord that we are made perfect, for we can do nothing on our own. By the Spirit of God (the Holy Ghost) by which we minister, heal the sick, raise the dead, and cast out demons, our flesh profits nothing (see John 6:63).

Your gift does not save apart from the anointing of the Spirit of God. Therefore, it's impossible for you to know yourself without Jesus Christ and the Father. If you know Jesus, then you know the Father also, and if you know the Father, you will learn yourself.

However, it is more important that Jesus know you more than you know Him.

"Strive to enter in at the strait gate: for many, I say unto you, will seek to enter in, and shall not be able. When once the master of the house is risen up, and hath shut to the door, and ye begin to stand without, and to knock at the door, saying, Lord, Lord, open unto us; and he shall answer and say unto you, I know you not whence ye are: Then shall ye begin to say, We have eaten and drunk in thy presence, and thou hast taught in our streets. But he shall say, I tell you, I know you not whence ye are; depart from me, all ye workers of iniquity."

~ Luke 13:24-27

Chapter 4

THE MAN: WITHOUT GOD

Strip, a man down to his bare soul and all he is left with, is a choice. He has a choice to die with nothing but his soul, or the choice to grow on from there and reach for higher heights than where he currently finds himself.

However, when you look at the things upon the earth which men can strive for, what does he actually obtain that he can take with him when his body dies? For all the things which man strives for, breaking his back to accomplish, using his time and energy to build; what of all of those can he actually account for when he dies?

His soul takes pride in his accomplishments, his degrees, the grand homes, cars, and bank accounts, but in the end he leaves all for another man to squander, plunder, and waste.

Yet for all this, the one thing or asset which he can take, or which will follow him to the grave and beyond; he rejects. He rejects it because it can't be measured, counted, or stacked in a room. It can't be put on display, hung on a nail, or in a display case as a trophy.

No one can readily see, acknowledge, or praise him for it; and that which he receives praises for, or acknowledgement for is a hoax, false, made to be seen,

A Man Like God

heard and praised as something he brings attention to; as if to say "see what I've done".

Therefore, in the pride of his heart he lifts up his knowledge and his intellect, for what else does he really possess? However, what shall even remain of those, for his knowledge shall come to nothing.

The car and the home, for which he takes pride in obtaining, may not truly be his, if someone else owns the title and deed. He has bought into a false sense of ownership, wherefore, if he misses a payment the bank comes-a-knocking, or they remove him or the property which is rightfully theirs.

So of all the things a man says is his, what is actually his? What can he keep that he can say is truly his and no one else's?

Even his life, the breath he breathes, is not his, but he utilizes them only for the short time he is upon the earth. Then they return to the one who gave them.

Plays The Fool

"He that trusteth in his own heart is a fool: but whoso walketh wisely, he shall be delivered."
~ *Proverbs 28:26*

Man left to himself can only follow the imagination of his own heart, which we read in scripture is divisive, having taken on the nature of Satan. Yet man doesn't even possess his own thoughts, because most of what he thinks apart from God is a product of demons, as is written:

THE MAN: WITHOUT GOD

"Man's goings are of the LORD; how can a man then understand his own way?"

~Proverbs 20:24

The evil man commits are from the Devil, the lies he tells belong to the Devil; for the Devil is a liar and the father of it (see John 8:44). He gets angry and hurts, or murders someone which is the product of demons. Anger, jealousy, malice, envy, pride, all these are products of demons. He wars and terrorizes and takes credit for the aftermath, and yet even this is born of demons.

Therefore, all the pride man takes in doing mischief to each other is actually the inner workings of a demon influencing him to do so. The final act is man's doing for which he will be judged, but the thought originating the act is not.

The belief which states there is no God comes from demons, therefore, man can't even take ownership of many of his own belief systems because they are also devised from demons. Of course demons don't want men to know this, and keep their dealing, plots, and plan secret; making the man think he is in control when he really is not. In this manner, the man plays the fool, as written:

"The fool hath said in his heart, There is no God."

~Psalms 14:1

He plays the fool because he thinks when he doesn't believe in a God who created him; he is actually expressing his own thoughts. He may have bought into them, but they certainly didn't originate from him.

A Man Like God

Man's belief system mainly stems from thoughts, ideas, and situations which occur outside of him, which demons construct to direct his thoughts and men considers these things and makes a final decision on what he will believe.

Which of us by taking thought and considering all the things which give us pleasure, would not make the decision to engage in them? After all it's fun, enjoyable, gives us pleasure, makes us feel good, helps us forget our troubles, and in the case of frequent sexual escapades; boosts our ego. Therefore, many of the things demons use against us are the things we find pleasurable, exciting, sociable, and thrilling.

God is seen as a strict parent making us miss out on what we consider the fun of life. Therefore, the laws and commandments which govern them are tempted and tried by men to test how far they can go in their disobedience before judgment falls.

In the Body of Christ many risks daily their salvation for just a moment of forbidden pleasure. Lusting and desiring things which we know God does not delight in. Living a secret lifestyle away from the crowd; after all who is going to know what we do in the privacy of our own home? Therefore, we maintain forbidden friendship, acquaintance, and fellowships.

Deceived by the fact that those around us who befriends us really support us in the things we do, and we keep those who would challenge us, confront us, and expose us at arm's length never allowing them to get too close.

THE MAN: WITHOUT GOD

In this, we play the fool again, not understanding it does not matter if man sees us; God sees us, and in due season he will judge, for it must be that judgment begin at the house of God (see 1 Peter 4:17).

Therefore, Adam finds himself in a precarious situation, having been put out of the Garden, facing a cruel world essentially on his own, with new rules and regulations which he is not accustomed to. Not understanding he is under a system which is bent on his destruction. The harmony of God is gone; the intimate, close, touchable love of God has dissipated. All is left is the insecurity he now feels being left with only his thoughts, and a demon poised to take advantage of it all.

For without God we are lost, contrived, and detrimental to our own selves. If we don't allow the architect of our being access to direct, lead, purpose, and build our lives then we are simply a mound of flesh hasting to our death; for without God we are dead while we live.

Is Self-Willed

"For men shall be lovers of their own selves, covetous, boasters, proud, blasphemers, disobedient to parents, unthankful, unholy, Without natural affection, trucebreakers, false accusers, incontinent, fierce, despisers of those that are good, Traitors, heady, highminded, lovers of pleasures more than lovers of God; Having a form of godliness, but denying the power thereof: from such turn away."
~2 Timothy 3:2-5

Stubbornness is one of the traits which many would say is imbedded in the heart of every man. Scripture bearing witness to this:

A Man Like God

"Every way of a man is right in his own eyes: but the LORD pondereth the hearts."

~Proverbs 21:2

The Merriam-Webster Dictionary defines stubbornness as unreasonably or perversely unyielding.

In other words; one who must have their way or its the highway. Sounds like many of the pastors and leaders we know today, who are so power-hungry, they would enslave God's people rather than give them the freedom God gives to obey, or disobey without casting or preaching them immediately into hell for their noncompliance.

Oppressing many of the children of God to be condemned, ostracized, and criticized for not following a particular leader to the letter of their law, using scripture to beat into submission God's heritage; instead of allowing God to deal with His children on His terms.

Men who are so determined to go their own way, they overlook the experience of experienced leaders who came before them, and are able to foresee the danger ahead. Willing to marry someone who they know is not good for them for the sake of marriage, simply because "I" want to have sex and marriage is the legal way to have it.

Self-willingness and stubbornness led many down a road which was not convenient or the will of God, causing many to be left hurt or dead, because they didn't want to listen to anyone about anything.

THE MAN: WITHOUT GOD

There are many who will be cast into hell, sinner and saint alike simply because they don't want to follow, or be in subjection to anyone.

Too many of our young people locked up behind bars, strung out on drugs, sick from disease, or dead because of their stubbornness and selfish ways; willing to pay the ultimate price to have it their way.

Well, we can't have it our way and go back with Jesus. We can't engage in sin and think there will be no consequences. There's no way to be happy while making others miserable, and there is no hope without God.

Self-willingness got Lucifer kicked out of heaven, Adam to curse a world full of men, and Cain to murder his brother. Self-will keeps you engaged in the self-fulfilling lust of your flesh, cheating on your wife, destroying the trust of your friend(s), and in danger of hell fire.

Self-will, the motivating force behind fights and arguments, and men killing each other because we will not allow ourselves to be talked about spat upon, lied to or on, betrayed, belittled, or defrauded.

We just can't allow anyone to gain the upper hand over us, and we remain transfixed on protecting, and saving our own lives when the Lord said:

"*Vengeance is mine, I will repay says the Lord.*"

~Romans 12:19

To be self-willed is to be prideful and we all know pride comes before destruction (see Proverbs 18:12).

A Man Like God

The pride which keeps us engaging in sinful pleasures because we don't think we will get caught.

The Devil devised a cunning method to keep man away from God, by uplifting himself in his own eyes. We must be careful to always remember that without God we are nothing.

Worships Strange Gods

"I am the LORD thy God, which have brought thee out of the land of Egypt, out of the house of bondage. Thou shalt have no other gods before me."

~Exodus 20:2-3

The fundamental thing which man does not want to understand, or comprehend is he was built, manufactured, created, and programmed to worship. If he does not worship God, he will worship something.

We witness this in the way men worship sports, cars, women, false gods, deities, and even themselves.

Man possesses the potential to become so engrossed in whatever he deems worthy, to love a thing or person even more than himself; worship is born out of love, for if he loves a thing he has no problem going great distances to express, or prove his love.

Why was it easy for Israel to leave the God who brought them out of Egypt, parted the Red Sea, fed them manna from heaven, drew water from a rock, and led them by a cloud during the day and a pillar of fire by night? To worship the gods of the lands which He commanded them not to worship, or fear?

THE MAN: WITHOUT GOD

I suppose it was easy for the same reason it's easy for us to turn back to the things we once were cleansed from; to take pleasure in our own flesh. It is so easy to relax and express the filth of the flesh, rather than be disciplined and obey the commandments of God. As revealed by scripture:

"*As a dog returneth to his vomit, so a fool returneth to his folly.*"

~Proverbs 26:11

The worship of other gods is easy because they don't demand of us the stringent obedience God does. The only requirement in worshipping false gods is to pleasure ourselves, because we make the rules which will govern how these gods or deities will be worshipped.

Not only gods but we also worship sex. Men worship sex and their own sex organs with a passion; many touching themselves constantly, unable to avoid even the minute opportunities to engage in sexual escapades, even to the destruction of family, ministry, work, or even their own lives.

Chasing women or men who ever they prefer with such fervor they are willing to risk being exposed in parks, stairwells, and even public restrooms. All for the worship of flesh, sex, and thrills.

Anything, everything, all things can be a god in our eyes. Idol worship is ramped even in our so-called house of worship; many worshipping the building, the artwork in the building, the pulpit, the pastor, and pulpit furniture. The worship of television shows, porn,

A Man Like God

internet, you name it and someone has possibly made a god out of it.

We never come to the understanding that our soul craves to worship its creator God. God the Father is still in our DNA, and sooner or later the soul will yearn to be in His presence.

This is why many are depressed, melancholy, and despondent because we are not feeding our spirit what it truly needs; the love of God by Jesus Christ.

CHAPTER 5

THE MAN: CHILD

"Children's children are the crown of old men; and the glory of children are their fathers."
~ *Proverbs 17:6*

Oh, what joy there must've been in the Adam's household when the first male child ever born to a woman, was born through Eve. Oh, how excited Adam must've been to see his first born son, how proud he must have been to hold Cain in his arms, dance him upon his knees, and carry him on his shoulders.

Who could've known or even imagined Cain, Adam's first born would grow up to be a murder? I am sure out of all the dreams and goals Adam had in mind for his son murderer was not one of them.

What happened in Cain's life as a child which would make him grow up with such hatred and disdain for his younger brother Able, which would make him rise up against him and kill him?

No doubt this same question has been asked by many parents today, who wonder how their son could've made such bad decisions and end up in prison, hooked on drugs, or dead.

What would've happened if Adam didn't sacrifice paradise for Eve? How different Cain would've been having never known good or evil, simply to exist without jealousy or envy, and Able may still be alive.

A Man Like God

Unfortunately, this was not to be, and now children are born knowing good and evil, and will mostly choose the evil rather than the good; needing to be taught by their parents to choose the good. An extremely hard task when the parents themselves haven't learned to choose the good rather than the evil. Nor learned that in Christ we have been made the righteousness of Jesus; and, therefore, no longer have the nature of Satan.

We don't have to listen to the ranting's of demon spirits, but mostly followed our own mind which possess the potential to be influenced by either Satan or Jesus. However, even the Body of Christ has mostly been influenced by demon spirits; to choose our own fleshly desires instead of the peace of God. This we've passed on to our children.

THE PROMISE OF A SON

"And I will bless her, and give thee a son also of her: yea, I will bless her, and she shall be a mother of nations; kings of people shall be of her."

~Genesis 17:16

For Abraham, the birth of a son would mark the beginning of the promise made to him by God, to establish him as the Father of many nations. A promise which to Abraham seemed impossible with him being one hundred years old, and Sarah being ninety, but we know and Abraham soon found out that there is nothing impossible to God.

"Then Abraham fell upon his face, and laughed, and said in his heart, Shall a child be born unto him that is an hundred years old? and shall Sarah, that is ninety years old, bear?"

~Genesis 17:17

THE MAN: CHILD

For many centuries the birth of a male child marked a time of celebration, and delight for the family. So much so even the first-born male among Israel (descendants of Abraham) was to be redeemed unto the Lord among the children of Israel:

*"And it came to pass, when Pharaoh would hardly let us go, that the LORD slew all the firstborn in the land of Egypt, both the firstborn of man, and the firstborn of beast: therefore I sacrifice to the LORD all that openeth the matrix (womb), being males; but all the firstborn of my children I redeem_*(in this case to restore to God)."

~Exodus 13:15 with emphasis added

Women who birthed male children for their husbands became women of status in the community. Those who were barren, or only had daughters, were ridiculed and ostracized by the other women in the community. So grievous was the ridicule to Hannah (who was barren) that she prayed to the Lord for a son and lent him to the Lord all the days of his life:

"And she said, Oh my lord, as thy soul liveth, my lord, I am the woman that stood by thee here, praying unto the LORD. For this child I prayed; and the LORD hath given me my petition which I asked of him: Therefore also I have lent him to the LORD; as long as he liveth he shall be lent to the LORD. And he worshipped the LORD there."

~1 Samuel 1:26-28

The Value of Male Children

The most famous fight of two women who competed for not only the love of their husband, but also to have the first born son, as well as many sons for

A Man Like God

their husband were Leah and Rachel, Jacob's (Israel) wives.

Male children were desired because they carried on the family line, the genealogy of families are carried accurately through the male.

It's the males who did the work in the fields, were the breadwinners so to speak, and protected the women from danger.

It would seem God was concerned with the male genealogy and only in certain cases did he name the mothers of the male children born, or the daughters born to those fathers.

God so created man as the head of the family even his ancestry (DNA) can be traced accurately through the Y Chromosomes of the male (only males carry the Y chromosomes), which passes from father to son virtually unchanged.

There are two methods of tracing lineage: **Paternal** and **Maternal**:

- **Paternal Lineage Test**: Analyzes specific segments of the Y-chromosome which is only found in males. And because the Y-chromosome is passed largely unchanged from father to son, DNA results from a male participant today can be used to represent the paternal lineage dozens of generations into the past.
- **Maternal Lineage Test**: Differs from the Paternal test in that it cannot validate a family relationship -- so even if your maternal DNA is an identical match with another participant it can only prove that you may have been related thousands of years ago. On the other hand, if your results differ in any way, the results prove that you are definitively not related. The Maternal Lineage test

THE MAN: CHILD

traces your ancient ancestry from your Mother's side. (From the Ancestry.com/DNA website)

Therefore, the value of a son was much valued to a father as well as to the community; for it was the males who carried the story of their lineage throughout their generations, as well as the relationship between God, gods, or deity worship.

The Head Even in Blood

Adam was quite excited about the birth of his two sons, not only because they were boys, but I'm sure he was happy he would finally receive help with the daily chores he once had to do alone.

The male child is valued because he alone carries the lineage of his family. A family's name can live for generations carried through the sons of fathers throughout a generation's lifetime.

In recent years mothers without fathers chose to continue their family name by giving their sons their last name, and not the last name of the father. What this does is discontinue the father's name throughout the generations of this child. However, God left a marker of the father in the DNA of the child, and if the son so desires to find out where he truly comes from; it's all in his blood.

Therefore, it doesn't matter if the father denies the existence of a child, if the father denies his prodigy; the blood will speak out at the judgment, and whosoever did not take responsibility for their lineage will bear their iniquity. Remember the scripture:

A Man Like God

"But if any provide not for his own, and specially for those of his own house, he hath denied the faith, and is worse than an infidel."

~1Timothy 5:8

By this, we understand God is not pleased when men who fulfilled their lust with a woman (without protection) deny the possibility of fathering a child. Therefore, in order to protect one's self from adverse judgment latter, it behooves a man to make sure he didn't father a child by having a DNA test done to clear his name, and his guilt. If he is found to have fathered a child, he should be responsible and take care of the child or children he fathered.

Men, we've been too supportive of men who do not take responsibility for their children, and continue to father more children. We as well as they retain much blood on our hands because we've partaken in these men sin. The blood of these children will speak out against us in the end.

THE BLOOD SPEAKS

"And he said, What hast thou done? the voice of thy brother's blood crieth unto me from the ground."
~Genesis 4:10

Lifted by his pride, Cain thought he got away from any guilt in killing his brother. However, he did not know that even in death the blood of his brother Able would continue to speak out, and God would hear his cry for justice.

In this way and for far too long, many men in their own pride allowed their sexual lust, in what seems to be

THE MAN: CHILD

some secret male code, to engage in sex with many partners, dropping children, and seemingly believing it is not their responsibility to raise or even be responsible for the children they fathered.

Therefore, many women who've been left by men after hearing they were pregnant committed abomination to having abortions, because they didn't feel they could take care of a child alone. These not only brought blood upon their own heads, but also on the fathers who left them to take on this responsibility alone. Therefore, a man whose child has been aborted is as guilty as the women who actually went through with the abortion.

In the judgment when the blood of these children speaks, God will cause both the woman and the man to be found guilty unless you repent, and stop this abominable behavior.

How many children are you inadvertently the murders of, because you couldn't bring yourself to take responsibility for your actions? How much blood is on your hands, and the cry of the blood of those children reached up to God, in that you gloried in your lust, rather than obeying the commandment of God? Will the blood of those children cry out against you?

Repent and turn from your lustful, promiscuous, and prideful ways so the Lord can wipe your sin away by His blood; which will speak to justify you when you turn from your own ways.

You retain the responsibility (being you may have had one night stands that have produced a child) to verify you didn't produce children with the women you slept with.

Why does the world's government need to make you responsible, when the Lord Jesus gave witness that you would be held responsible:

"For we must all appear before the judgment seat of Christ; that every one may receive the things done in his body, according to that he hath done, whether it be good or bad."

~2 Corinthians 5:10

THE MOLDING OF A MAN

"Train up a child in the way he should go: and when he is old, he will not depart from it."

~Proverbs 22:6

My mind goes back to reading in Genesis how God formed man with His own hands; taking much care to mold in his own image a man whom He had lived with in His Spirit from the foundation of the Earth. God Himself breathing into his nostrils His own spirit and causing man to become a living soul. Man was created in the image and nature of the one and only God.

Wow that makes me want to run down the street screaming: "I am fearfully and wonderfully made!"

The Nature of God

I am not sure we really understand what it means to be created in the image of God. Not only the image of God but the nature of God which must cause us to consider: "What is the Nature of God?"

THE MAN: CHILD

"But the wisdom that is from above is first pure, then peaceable, gentle, and easy to be intreated, full of mercy and good fruits, without partiality, and without hypocrisy."

~James 3:17

We understand wisdom comes from God; therefore, the wisdom of God is God as much as the Word of God is God. From the scripture above, we understand God's wisdom (nature) is first pure.

According to the Merriam-Webster dictionary, pure means to be free from dust, dirt, or taint: free from what vitiates (to debase in moral or aesthetic status), weakens, or pollutes: containing nothing that does not properly belong.

Therefore, we can understand the nature of God contains nothing which will weaken, pollute, debase makes unclean or filthy; all which sin does. Sin no longer belongs in our nature, because we are no longer born of sin (nature of Satan). Therefore, if sin reigns or rules in our mortal flesh, we are not exhibiting the nature of God, our creator.

The nature of God is peaceable: "

If it be possible, as much as lieth in you, live peaceably with all men."

~Romans 12:18

Merriam-Webster dictionary defines peaceable as not contentious or quarrelsome; quietly behaved; free from strife or disorder.

We have eliminated most of the Body of Christ with this one, because we can't help being all of which has been described as not being peaceable.

A Man Like God

Many men in the Body of Christ have made up their mind that they will not allow anyone to demean or mistreat them; therefore, in order to combat this, they act in the opposite of peace in order to defend themselves. Man's reputation is enmity against God, because a man's reputation will cause him to act unseemly to defend it.

"Now therefore there is utterly a fault among you, because ye go to law one with another. Why do ye not rather take wrong? Why do ye not rather suffer yourselves to be defrauded?"

~1 Corinthians 6:7

The nature of God is to be easily entreated (easy to deal with), full of mercy; which means to have compassion or forbearance shown especially to an offender or to one subject to one's power. The nature of God produces good fruits, without partiality, and without hypocrisy.

These are the characteristics which should be in man as well as being groomed in the young men born to parents in the Body of Christ. However, is the nature of God being groomed in our young men, or the nature of Satan?

An Adverse Nature

If God's nature is peaceable, merciful, pure, easily to be entreated, produces good fruits, not having partiality, or hypocrisy, shouldn't we also raise our sons with these same characteristics? For God told us to train up our children in the way, they should go (see Proverbs 22:6).

THE MAN: CHILD

There is a stark difference between how children were raised back in the day (to use a street vernacular), and how they are raised today.

One of the main issues is, we take pride in raising our children in church, but we don't raise them in God. Meaning we do not train them to have a relationship with God. Long as they are in worship service and they go to Sunday school we say they are good, or we have completed our duty in making sure they attend worship service.

I remember when my son got to be about 17 years old; he wasn't as excited about going to worship services as he used to be. Therefore, I asked the Lord concerning this, and the Lord answered me: "You raised him in church, but not in God." I was devastated, because I realized at that moment I had acquainted having him in worship service as also teaching him how to develop a relationship with the Lord.

Therefore, many think because they take or send their children to worship service and they know the order of service, or even can quote whole Psalm chapters this means they have a relationship with the Lord. As I have learned; nothing could be farther from the truth.

Then when they come of age they stop wanting to attend worship services on a regular basis, because we gave them "church", but we didn't give them Jesus.

On the other hand, many parents sent their children to worship service or Sunday school, but didn't foster a relationship with the Lord in their own lives; therefore, the children went to the worship service and learned a

A Man Like God

few dos and don'ts, but when they got home all they witnessed were the don't. With this, they took on the adverse nature of Satan, rather than the nature of God, because they learned church, but they didn't learn the nature of God or what God expected of them.

Through this we now have a nation of people who went or go to worship service, but didn't or don't appear before God so the intent of their hearts may be corrected. Through this lack of relationship with Christ, we now live with prayer taken out of schools, sons who'd rather be on the street corners, in prison, or on drugs because we gave them 'church', but no God.

Our sons are angry, despondent, hurt, dismayed, feel unloved, possess no compassion, no real desire for much, and are whores and whoremongers. All because we fathers thought it was more important to keep them in 'church', but not foster a relationship with God.

Mainly because we thought they were too young, they wouldn't understand, so we didn't let them in the room with us when we prayed, they hardly see us in the midst of the congregation worshipping the Lord. Therefore, they don't understand how to worship or they receive their lesson in worship from women.

They know how to act as though they are worshipping, or praising the Lord, but they don't know what it means to really and truly have a relationship with the Lord.

What does it mean to pray and expect God to move on my behalf? What does it mean to worship and praise God in spirit and truth? What are you doing when you speak in tongues? Children learn by example; what is

THE MAN: CHILD

the example we are setting before them in our daily worship?

Therefore, for many parents their children are unruly, complacent, seeking joy from drugs and sex, and these are children born to parents of the Kingdom.

How can we teach them how to obey God if we are constantly disobeying God? How can we tell them to abstain from sex before marriage when we have children all over the state, or are being exposed having sex against the plan of God?

How can we help them take on the nature of God, when we are constantly displaying the nature of Satan?

If you are cussing in the midst of the home, why do you expect them not to? They may learn to speak the Devil's language, and be promiscuous, but they should not be learning it from you Dad.

GOD'S CHILD REARING PLAN

Unfortunately, sin is contained in us at birth because Adam sinned against God in the Garden, causing sin upon all flesh. Therefore, everyone born of a woman already possesses within them the capacity to sin, or exude the nature of Satan.

This, however, was never the plan of God. His plan included us never to know good or evil, pain or suffering, or any of the many adverse things we experience today. His plan included peace, and joy all the days of our life.

Now we are encumbered with sin, and Satan's desire to keep us in this state for eternity, but God's given us a

A MAN LIKE GOD

way out through the death, burial, and resurrection of Jesus Christ. We do not need to remain in the nature of Satan, but can freely receive again the nature of God by Jesus Christ.

We understand this is salvation in the name of Jesus Christ, and all flesh need to have a savior. Once we embrace Jesus as our Lord and savior, it is God's plan that we also teach our children to also embrace the love of Jesus, and walk out their own salvation through the acceptance of Jesus as their personal savior.

Therefore, we must begin to teach them the commandments, behaviors, expectations of God from birth. God said train them up in the way they should go. Which means as they are growing up we should be training them in the things of God?

Just as you need to see a move of God in your life, they need to see a move of God in their life as well. Just like you need to see God answering your prayers, they need to see their prayers being answered as well.

If you must obey the Word of God, they must obey it as well. Do not look upon their age, because they won't always be this cute.

We fathers and men are the catalyst and it must start with us. We are the lawgivers and we must be the ones to enforce with our wives how the home will be run. If we are truly going to serve the Lord in our house, everything in the house must serve the Lord.

When Nineveh heard the prophesy of Jonah, the king of Nineveh made this declaration:

THE MAN: CHILD

"For word came unto the king of Nineveh, and he arose from his throne, and he laid his robe from him, and covered him with sackcloth, and sat in ashes. And he caused it to be proclaimed and published through Nineveh by the decree of the king and his nobles, saying, Let neither man nor beast, herd nor flock, taste any thing: let them not feed, nor drink water: But let man and beast be covered with sackcloth, and cry mightily unto God: yea, let them turn everyone from his evil way, and from the violence that is in their hands. Who can tell if God will turn and repent, and turn away from his fierce anger, that we perish not?"

~Jonah 3:6-9

The king of Nineveh had everyone in his kingdom fast which also included the children, he let none taste food or water, but had them all cry out to God for mercy. This is our example of what we as fathers must do if we desire our children to come up in the way they should go.

God told Moses: *"Therefore shall ye lay up these my words in your heart and in your soul, and bind them for a sign upon your hand, that they may be as frontlets between your eyes. And ye shall teach them your children, speaking of them when thou sittest in thine house, and when thou walkest by the way, when thou liest down, and when thou risest up."*

~Deuteronomy 11:18-19

Moses began to teach the children of Israel the law before his death, admonishing them to take heed to the things the Lord commanded them. Informing them to teach their children the law as they sat at the dinner table, or when they walked where ever they went. Even

A Man Like God

as they sat in their houses they were instructed to teach their children the law.

How much time do we spend teaching our children the Word of God they are also to keep? Are they in front of the TV, video game, or on the computer more than they are hearing the Word of God which can save their souls?

We must reconsider how we are raising our children. What examples are we setting, by compromising the Word of God simply because they are our children and underage? We are partly to blame for the way our children are in this world today.

> *"But when Jesus saw it, he was much displeased, and said unto them, suffer the little children to come unto me, and forbid them not: for of such is the kingdom of God."*
> ~Mark 10:14

COME OUT FROM AMONG THEM.

Much of what we are dealing with is because we have allowed our children to attend schools which put no value on Biblical commandments, or Biblical truth.

Our children leave our homes where we may be teaching them Biblical values, and they go to a system which teaches the opposite of what is being discussed in the home. A godless system which teaches word recognition without comprehension of what those words mean.

Therefore, our children get conflicting messages, because they get one thing at home and another from their peers. It is important we keep our children in a school system that will value our way of life. We must

THE MAN: CHILD

develop schools which will keep God at the forefront, and monitor the images our children are seeing on a daily basis closely.

I recommend we develop our own schools (as many have done) which will keep our children together under a God-centered program, where they learn to pray, worship, walk before the Lord, as well as reading, writing, and arithmetic.

The Devil is destroying the education system of the world in order to destroy our children in the process. How many of our children need to be shot, or face the fear of being shot in the public school system, because they will not recognize the need of God back in the schools.

If we as children of God must come out from among the world, why do we send our children into the world to learn? Therefore, why are we surprised when our children come home with ungodly desires and habits when we force them to sit in an environment where these things are birthed?

It is time we take complete responsibility and authority of how our children are being taught out of our presence. Time for us fathers to get back involved in the Godly rearing of our children; then we can stop complaining about the flawed system.

"What is man, that thou art mindful of him? and the son of man, that thou visitest him?"

~Psalm 8:4

Chapter 6

MAN

A unique specimen man is, capable of extraordinary passions, and immense cruelty; able to exhibit the most wondrous care and yet, kill without any regret. He is a constant contradiction within himself as he carries the pain of his childhood, physical abuse, molestations, self-hatred, pride, anger, wrath, lust, and for some; the absence of a father figure.

He's been taught to deny his own feelings keep a stiff upper lip, do not show any weakness, and certainly don't shed a tear.

Therefore, he learns to hide his emotions to keep them buried remembering the lessons his mother taught him; "Big boys don't cry." Yet he marries and his wife tells him: "You don't show any emotions."

A conflicted life he leads having to juggle prayerfully a loving wife, family, friends, work and play, and still remain a man's man in the end. Man has learned to keep a smile on his face while he is dying inside, and no one knows it until he kills himself, or someone else.

When he is a child he is faced with finding his own identity in a sea of boys, who don't know who they are, who clamor to find their place in the world stepping over anyone in the process; as crabs in a bucket pulling down one another in the process.

A Man Like God

He tries to find himself in a world where image is everything, and if he doesn't look the part he is ostracized, criticized, belittled, and cast aside.

He is held to be the strong one, while being reminded of how weak he really is. He is honored and despised, loved and hated; needed and unwanted he is MAN.

THE FORMATIVE YEARS

"Train up a child in the way he should go: when he is old, he will not depart from it."

~Proverbs 22:6

The formative years, the time when young boys turn into young men, when their bodies change into the likeness of a man and their voices now has some bass to it.

These are the years when he becomes the man he will always be. He's grown from the babe needing the attention of his parent(s) constantly, to the adolescent who needs less attention, into a young adult who is now thinking about moving away from home, to college, job, and career.

By now he's developed his own way of thinking and operating, his own core beliefs, and his own way of viewing the world. Based on his experience thus far, he will make decisions, form opinions, and decide if his parent's views or beliefs will be his own.

Depending on his upbringing, sex and relationship are now the new frontiers he will need to conquer, or be trampled under.

MAN

The school yard crush is gone, and he comes face to face with real relationships, possibly for the first time. What he has seen and experienced as a child will play a great role in how he interacts with his partner. His character will determine if he is a faithful partner, or one who plays around with multiple partners.

The young man comes face to face with the question of his sexual preference many times, contemplating and maybe even experimenting with same sex relationships, and deciding he is heterosexual, homosexual, or bi-sexual; each one having its own difficulty, joy, and anguish, and one of them will cause him to hide and fulfill his desire secretly (Men on the Down-Low). Even marrying to keep his true desires a secret, and wounding an innocent life in the process.

Again, based on his upbringing and his influences he has a relationship with church, personal relationship with Christ or no belief in God at all.

Man bears an image of himself and an image that others place on him, and trying to juggle the two becomes a constant fight. Although he's been taught to be self-sufficient he longs for the gratification that comes from being able to depend on someone.

Depending upon whether he received (in his opinion) enough love and support from his parents, family, and friends as a child; he may be overly dependent upon others, independent and prideful or independent to the point of living a solitary life.

These are the years in which men dispel many of the things society, his parents, and family taught him; or

A Man Like God

cleave to them with the fervor of a man desperately holding on to his most precious possessions.

It is now when a young man begins to experience life without the safety net of his parents. His success or failures are his and his alone. The mistakes made are his to blame others for, or to take the consequences of.

He is a young adult male who has been dreaming of this moment for most of his preteen and teen existence. This is when pride comes in and causes him to reject the wisdom of those who came before him. It is now (if he was raised in a God-fearing home) where he begins to do most of the things he was not allowed to do in his parent's home.

Freedom can be a crippling thing if not used wisely.

Men After Our Own Kind

"For we dare not make ourselves of the number, or compare ourselves with some that commend themselves: but they measuring themselves by themselves, and comparing themselves among themselves, are not wise."

~2 Corinthians 10:12

What makes a man a man in the eyes of a woman and in the eyes of a man are two different things.

Women for the most part see men as the breadwinners, the protector, rough and ruddy, crass, masculine, and not a crybaby (stereotypical I know). Therefore, for him to show any emotion is a weakness in her eyes. However, she also complains about the rough exterior, the lack of emotion, and the utter disregard most men exude for her emotional way of being.

MAN

Men carry what I call an unspoken man code which we are taught from birth. Men don't expect a man to be weak, cry, and talk a lot. He's expected to enjoy sports and be athletic, to enjoy many sexual partners, to lose his virginity at an early age, and to work until his day is done.

In the eyes of his male peers he is counted as weak and gay if he is very sensitive, is yet a virgin and does not chase women. Should he be found unable to fight, he is ridiculed and many times pushed into fighting in the unscrupulous attempt to make him more of a man.

In whatever way a man is perceived to be a man all of it is based on man's views; his thoughts, his prejudices, his personal view of what constitutes a man. None of, or very little of which is based on the God, who created him.

We go around placing our own personal invisible signs on God's creation, whom we deem to be men or not. All based on a warped since of what we think a man should be.

Much of what we think a man should be is not based on the nature of God, who created him, but on the nature of demons who seek to destroy him.

Society says a man simply is a man when he flirts, or is having sex with multiple partners. God told man not to commit fornication (sex out of wedlock) and not covet (to lust upon or after). He is a man when he goes out and engages in sex with someone other than his wife (adultery); God said man should not commit adultery.

Being men created in the image and likeness of God, we consistently base our manhood on an existence

A Man Like God

which is not molded after the image of God at all. Do we think God, who possessed the power to create man in His own image, doesn't also retain the power to mold us in His image?

However, looking at ourselves and comparing our manhood among ourselves is not wise.

SPIRIT NOT FLESH

"And the Lord God formed man of the dust of the ground, and breathed into his nostrils the breath of life; and man became a living soul."

~Genesis 2:7

The Free Dictionary lists two definitions of Soul:

1) The spiritual nature of humans, regarded as immortal, separable from the body at death, and susceptible to happiness or misery in a future state.

2) The disembodied spirit of a dead human.

In fact, the soul of man is what God breathed into Adam in the Garden of Eden. Man therefore, is inherently spirit and not flesh. The body was created to carry the soul around and to keep man tethered to the earth.

God created the man a body which was suited to the environment of earth, and would allow him to interact with his environment.

What causes us to be flesh is our mindset not that we live in a building of flesh. Therefore, if you think of yourself as a man simply and naively based on the fact that you have male genitalia; you've missed the essence of what God created completely.

Image and Likeness of God

Man was man long before God placed him in a clay shell. God said "let us make man in our image and in our likeness (see Genesis 1:26)," therefore man had to be a spirit first in order to be in God's image and likeness because God is a spirit.

When babies are born, they are born in the image and likeness of their parents. This means that they have (hopefully) ten fingers, ten toes, two legs, two arms, one-head, and the section which conceals their vital organs which makeup the body. If not we call them abnormal.

Afore God created man a body on earth, he was already made in the image of God, this signified by the fact God coughed the man up out of Himself and breathed him into the form He created, and then man became a living Soul. Therefore, the image of God is not the shell without, but the soul within.

Adam understood this and was able to live out his days before his fall without being sexually motivated. Without the need for sex frequently and regularly; to which we contribute to being a man.

It wasn't until Adam disobeyed the Lord, eating the fruit he was commanded not to eat, that he became susceptible to the devil's mental stimuli of lust and covetousness. He also lost his spirit mentality and took on the mentality of demons.

A Man Like God

"And it came to pass, when men began to multiply on the face of the earth, and daughters were born unto them. That the sons of God saw the daughters of men that they were fair, and they took them wives of all which they chose."

~Genesis 6:1-2

Many will say the reference to the "sons of God" in the passage above is speaking of angels who came down in the likeness of men, and married women. However, this scripture not only reference angels, but also men who through their lust birthed through the devil, began to look upon women with lust filled eyes, and took of them to wife as many as they pleased. This bearing witness, they were not satisfied with just one wife but burned in their lust and left the order of God being influenced by the devil and his demons.

To which God said:

"My spirit shall not always strive with man, for that he also is flesh: yet his days shall be an hundred and twenty years."

~Genesis 6:3

"For that he also is flesh." God is not speaking about the body here, but that man being spirit now begins to practice that which is made alive in the flesh through demon influence. What you practice you become.

Man has now cast down his spirit nature, and taken on the nature of Satan to which God will no longer strive with him.

To strive means to struggle or fight vigorously with. Therefore, God was saying I will not always struggle and fight with the man to cause him to walk after my

MAN

way, or his true nature. He has tasted of the forbidden fruit (sin) and transfixed his heart to follow after it.

God extended man the gift of choice and will not fight with him to make a different choice. For God already said through Moses:

"I call heaven and earth to record this day against you, that I have set before you life and death, blessings and cursing: therefore choose life, that both thou and they seed may live."

~Deuteronomy 30:19

It is your choice to choose life or death, and God, or Jesus will not fight your decision.

IDENTITY CRISIS

"Man's going are of the LORD: how can a man then understand his own way?"
~*Proverbs 20:24*

Man as a whole is now dealing with an identity crisis because he's established himself as a man in the nature of Satan, attempting to live out the nature of God. Refusing to acknowledge the fact he is the image of God, whom Jesus has redeemed back to God, and receive once more communion with the Spirit of God (if filled with the Holy Ghost) or the mindset of God dwelling within him; still he makes the choice to walk out the nature of Satan.

We do not sin because we are in the body because we've already proven we are spirit without a body. If the body cannot live without a soul, then the body is not man, but the soul within the body is man; making man a spirit not flesh.

A Man Like God

Therefore, man is a spirit, but his spirit has been overshadowed by demons which cloud the understanding of his true self.

The instant Adam ate the fruit he gave Satan license to play with our minds, and cause us to go a whoring after the things which God hates; in an attempt to separate us from God to destroy the image of God in the Earth.

Satan's prime goal was not the casting down per say of a woman, but the man, because God gave man the authority and the dominion upon Earth. So Satan went to the woman because he understood Adam like Jesus, would sacrifice himself for his wife as Christ sacrificed Himself for His Church. Therefore, woman is not the cause of man's bad decisions: man is.

Today man's bad decisions are still causing him to lose his dominion and authority. Satan touches his loins and he makes the decision to commit fornication, or adultery. The devil touches his emotions, and man is quick to anger which causes him to kill a man: all because of his identity crisis.

Man doesn't know who he is; therefore, he crashes into trouble and destruction as a drunken man high on booze or crack-cocaine without a thought of the consequences or regard of who gets hurt.

The brother who is saved and filled with the Holy Ghost is dealing with an identity crisis, because he doesn't know, nor understand he is no longer of the nature of Satan, but is redeemed to his original nature which was created in the image and likeness of God, the Father.

MAN

In order to redeem something a price must be paid, in this case the price was the life of Jesus Christ.

Too many of God sons are performing heinous acts because they are living out the nature of Satan while attempting to walk out the nature of God. This is a man with an identity crisis.

The Fundamentals

Man is spirit not flesh. The curse of Adam caused him to lose his identity and relationship with God; causing him to act out the nature of Satan rather than his true nature which is of God.

The world's view of manliness has become based on a cursed system instituted by demon spirits, whose only focus is the destruction of man and thereby the ill-fated belief they can overthrow God.

This he (Satan) does by influencing and stimulating mans' flesh, emotions, and five senses. Satan blinds man to the dangers of worldly pleasures causing him to engage in sex, drugs, alcohol, and greed; all which destroys the body in some way.

Whenever sex is performed outside of the commandment of God, it is destructive and defiles the body which is the temple of the Holy Ghost (you are only the temple of Holy Ghost if the Holy Ghost lives inside of you).

"If any man defile the temple of God, him shall God destroy; for the temple of God is holy, which temple ye are."

~1 Corinthians 3:17

A Man Like God

Please understand this; man is a spirit, always has been, and will always be a spirit. His mind and thoughts are what caused him to live, walk, and perform the nature of Satan (this is what God meant when he said: "man is also flesh" meaning his mind was turned from God). This is why mans' mind must be renewed:

"And be not conformed to this world: but be ye transformed by the renewing of your mind, that ye may prove what is that good, and acceptable, and perfect, will of God."

~Romans 12:2

What the mind thinks the body will do and what is conceived in the mind will corrupt the heart, which will in turn destroy the man.

Chapter 8

MAN: IN CRISIS

What is MAN? Does he even know himself? In Biblical terms one could say no, for it's stated:

"Man's goings are of the LORD; how can a man then understand his own way?"

~Proverbs 20:24

It was stated in a previous chapter that in order to understand the original plan for a thing you must go back to the original design, or manufacturer to fully understand its function.

Therefore, for a man to fully understand his purpose in the earth, he must go back to the original blueprint which is found in the first chapters of Genesis.

Is it the nature of man to be what he is today; self-willed, lustful, prideful, and arrogant? Was it God's plan that man should be angry, hateful, murderers, unable to truly love the image of himself, and despisers of those he considers weaker than himself?

Is God's plan for man to possess the inability to express love being created in the image of a God of love? To think it manly to walk around looking angry all the time, to glorify our loins more than we glorify God, or to chase after carnal pleasures (immoral sexual desires) and designate this as man's way?

We call it manly to have more than one sexual partner at a time, manly to fight and war, to destroy

A Man Like God

more than we build, and to take more than we give. Is this the original plan of God for man?

Let's consider the image of a man in the earth today: Even in the Body of Christ. He is looked upon as unfaithful being unable to deny his own lust which causes him to cheat on his wife, being leaders having sex in the congregation with both men and woman. He is not trustworthy or dependable in most cases (howbeit there are men who are truly faithful).

Man is in crisis because he goes about finding himself apart from God his creator, giving heed to his natural desires which are also the nature of Satan.

This author has heard many men say "it's natural for men to want sex often, to be confrontational, and defend one's self." However, what men call natural in the flesh is actually the nature of demon spirits being played out in man.

Therefore, again man is in crisis because he does not know the very thing in which he's grown attached and accustomed to in the flesh, are demon spirits which cause him to desire the things which God has told him to deny.

These things then are played out in the everyday lives of men, which cause strife, envy, anger, wrath, war, sedition, division, murder, hatred, imprisonment, slavery, whoredom, curses, and every evil work.

Somehow even our salvation today is obtained almost without God. We don't mind being sons of God as long as we don't actually have to be saved, as long as we don't have to give up anything, do much of

Man: In Crisis

anything, deny ourselves the pleasures of this world, or sacrifice anything for what we believe.

Holiness is a joke, yet we say we serve a Holy God. We don't mind you being saved, but don't become fanatical in your salvation. In other word, don't become what we term spooky, too spiritual, too holy, or make someone uncomfortable with your salvation.

We don't want to lose too much of the world, but we also don't want to gain too much of God.

Therefore, we settle for a mediocre relationship with the Lord, but we want a powerful demonstration of God. We men are in crisis.

Prideful

"Pride goeth before destruction, and an haughty spirit before a fall."
~Proverbs 16:18

Pride is an inflated sense of one's personal status or accomplishments. It can also show it's self in vanity or where a person is overly impressed with his own looks and physical appearance. Pride causes one to be inflated over their gifts, and resistant to needed help from others.

Pride may blind one from the truth and cause him to take unnecessary risks.

Not to be confused with confidence, pride causes an exasperated belief in self regardless of the evidence to the contrary. It is seen in the ill-fated belief that he doesn't need anyone, or to take the stance that he is God alone.

A Man Like God

The fall of many in the Body of Christ is the result of prideful men which the Lord has had to expose in order to humble those who lifted themselves in pride in His presence; those who continued in sin simply because God is a loving, merciful, and forgiving God; who delights not in the destruction of the wicked.

So puffed up by the attention they receive, they convinced themselves they are above the laws and rules which govern others. That somehow they will not receive the same judgments which all of the Body of Christ is subject to.

The devil has wielded pride like a weavers beam against man causing him to destroy himself because he can't see the true danger he is in.

This can be seen in the way man will defend himself in sin, demanding not to be judged by his peers for the wrong he continues to do, and foolishly stating: "God knows my heart."

Pride is present when we engage in the pleasures of this world, when we keep company with the unlawful, covenant breakers, whoremongers, and think there's nothing wrong.

Pride causes us to engage in sin, and walk into the congregation worshiping and praising as if we did nothing wrong.

The Body of Christ has been made blind through pride lusting after the fashion, music, and entertainment of this world. We've brought the devil's music into the congregation of the Lord, in an attempt to draw the world to the Lord.

Man: In Crisis

We've not understood that you can't transform people using the devil's stuff; it's men who sit in the pulpits of our assemblies and allow these things to go on (for the most part).

Men, who in pride have defiled our women, left our children destitute without fathers, and go a whoring after strange flesh.

We want to be in control, but can't even control ourselves. We want to obtain authority, but can't stand under the pressure of our own flesh. We want to be honored, but have yet to honor God with our whole mind, body, and spirit. We want to be known, but don't even know ourselves.

We are in crisis.

Pride, gentlemen made us weak while we think we are strong. It caused us to take confidence in that which is temporary and not eternal.

We stroke each other's egos, and bolstered our loins while we die internally.

Pride has brought down kingdoms, subdued countries, and destroyed nations. Don't let your own pride destroy you.

Wrath, Anger and Unforgiveness

"Judge not, and ye shall not be judged: condemn not, and ye shall not be condemned: forgive, and ye shall be forgiven."
~ Luke 6:37

To be hypocritical is to preach or teach something while doing something else: for example, to teach

A Man Like God

forgiveness while refusing to forgive others of their transgressions.

Men are known for their anger and unforgiving ways. You hear it over the pulpit when someone leaves the congregation without the permission of the pastor. You listen as they downgrade, demean, and polarize those who for one reason or another felt the need to leave.

We men pride ourselves on not being emotional, yet we are more emotional than we lead ourselves and others to believe.

Though we've been raised to show no emotions we show them all the time, albeit we are very selective with whom we show them to.

We've learned to show wrath and anger without restraint. In fact, it's even considered manly to show anger rather than love. This is why most of us walk around with our faces looking like we sucked on lemons and prunes all day.

We embrace anger, wrath, and un-forgiveness like a life jacket, refusing to show even a hint of kindness in the fear it makes us look weak.

When we embrace these we deny our true heritage which is locked in the bosom of a loving God. Why have we embraced anger, hatred, and un-forgiveness to be manly when the God who created us is none of these things?

Even when we are in love many of us will still show anger, or malice rather than kindness and love; and this you call being a man.

MAN: IN CRISIS

Anger, Wrath, and Un-forgiveness are the fruit of the enemy used to keep you from the love of a gracious, loving, and forgiving God.

God did not create you to be angry, hateful, or unforgiving. As you will see in the next section; God intended you to be as He is, and to be very free in expressing His love.

THE ORIGINAL PLAN

What then is the original plan for man? *"And God said, Let us make man in our image, after our likeness: and let them have dominion over the fish of the sea, and over the fowl of the air, and over the cattle, and over all the earth, and over every creeping thing that creepeth upon the earth."*

~ Genesis 1:26

From the scripture above we see God first desired to make man in His own image, His likeness, and to give him dominion.

The definition of image is an exact external likeness: a person looking strikingly like another person as in God. Likeness (after our likeness) speaks more about God's character meaning His nature, or the way in which He operates, and of course, dominion speaks of having authority, ruler-ship, and power.

Therefore, God intended man to not only look like Him, but act like Him, move like Him, do the things He does. Finally demonstrate power, authority, and sovereignty over the Earth. In other words, nothing can take place in this world without the express permission of man.

A Man Like God

Man possesses in Earth what Lucifer lusted for in Heaven, and what Satan now craves to keep. Therefore, as long as Satan can keep you in a lustful, sinful, ignorant state, he can steal all God intended for you.

God is love, therefore, He intended man to express love in the earth. However, when Adam sinned he caused men to take on the nature of Satan, and, therefore, caused hatred to be the call of the day.

This is why it is so hard for men to love from their heart, because Satan continually influences him to hate and despise his fellow man. In the absence of love hatred, anger, wrath, malice, and murder will breed.

This is why there is so much discord in the midst of our congregation, because greed has taken the place of love, and we go about vying for position, status, and prestige rather than Godly love and contentment.

God intended Earth to be another Heaven, but man turned away from God, and allowed Satan to influence him to deny God in his heart, and turn aside after Satan in the guise of fleshly (sinful) pleasure and greed.

Reestablishing The Original Plan

"If my people, which are called by my name, shall humble themselves, and pray, and seek my face, and turn from their wicked ways; then will I hear from heaven, and will forgive their sin, and will heal their land."

~ 2 Chronicle 7:14

In order to reestablish God's original plan for man we must turn away from our own way, and embrace God in His fullness. We must denounce the nature of

MAN: IN CRISIS

Satan and all his vices, deny ourselves, pick up our cross, and follow Jesus completely.

We as men must choose this day whom we will serve whether it will be our flesh (sinful, Satan nature) or Christ. We cannot continue to serve two masters. You cannot serve God and your flesh there has to be a choice made, and no choice is a choice.

It is written we should renounce the hidden things of dishonesty (see 2 Corinthians 4:2). Many men married attempting to hide their sexual desires for men, thinking if they are married no one will suspect them of having these unnatural desires. However, nothing is secret with God, for all things are open to him and nothing covered.

One of the issues with men is they continuously compare themselves among themselves. They are constantly attempting to build up men in their own image instead of the image of God. This is counterproductive in the Body of Christ, because the pattern we are to follow is not man, but God.

This brought about the saying amongst pastors and leaders: "We need to reproduce after our own kind." The problem with this is what we've reproduced is after our own kind. Therefore, if the leader is selfish, self-willed, self-serving, immoral, and sexually in error then what is produced in those who follow them is the same things (in most cases).

This is why we must build Christ in the hearts of men, so we are not producing ourselves, but Christ. This was the original plan of God, to have men on Earth who represent Him through and through, and then

A Man Like God

repeat that image throughout our generations. This is why Christ came, died and revived so He could give us the nature of God again, and that we could multiply that nature in all the Earth.

In order to reestablish God's original plan we must emulate Christ in every area of our lives, and not fulfill the lusts of the flesh and make excuses for why we do what we do.

Chapter 7

IN NEED OF A SAVIOR

The inability of a man to restore himself to the nature of God paved the way for God to reveal His plan to a dying world.

Man was incapable, or unwilling to change being totally at the mercy of a demon who could so manipulate him to forget God, while deceiving man of his (Satan's) own existence. Therefore, the things which men do is seen not as the influence of demon spirits, but his own will, desires, and emotions.

Mans' existence is purely based on self; self-gratification, self-identity, and self-pleasure; meaning as long as I get what I want, all is well with the world. Even the charity he does for the most part is in an attempt for self-gratification, to keep eyes on him and his great deed he has done.

We can recognize the need for children of their parents, the need for food, clothes, and shelter but can't seem to grasp our dire need of a savior. After we receive Jesus as our personal savior, some still stay tethered to sin, which is no longer their nature.

"But as he which hath called you is holy, so be ye holy in all manner of conversation; Because it is written, Be ye holy; for I am holy."

~1 Peter 1:15

Holy or holiness means to be free of sin as God is free of sin.

A Man Like God

The true nature of man has been tainted, polluted, diluted, and changed to reflect his own will and emotions; which is based on the nature of the father of lies (Satan).

The Father seeing this from Heaven, watching as the soul he detached from Himself dies every day. What else could a father do but seek to save his son who is lost.

Reason For A Savior

"And the LORD God said, Behold, the man is become as one of us, to know good and evil: and now, lest he put forth his hand, and take also of the tree of life, and eat, and live forever; Therefore the LORD God sent him forth from the garden of Eden, to till the ground from whence he was taken."
~ Genesis 3:22-23

Mans' birthright was stolen by deception and disobedience, causing men to be sold into the bondage of sin. Captured by Satan, denigrated (to deny the importance or validity of), polluted in the attempt to obliterate him from the planet.

Man's become a shadow of his former self. Dejected from the man who was king, having all authority and dominion in the earth, and sovereign in his ruler ship; to a man who is now subservient in the place he once ruled.

He's now become the opposite of who he was created to be. He is no longer the ruler of the land created just for him; sin, death and the grave are his rulers now, and they keep a vise grip on him refusing to let him go.

IN NEED OF A SAVIOR

It is amazing, the very things we think are exciting and joyful in the world are the very things Satan is using to destroy us, and he is using them in a manner which causes us to destroy ourselves. We are truly destroyed for lack of knowledge.

It must've been hard for God to see Himself in such a state.

The blood of goats and bulls (see Hebrews 10:4) cannot cause man to forget the bondage of sin, or make him become righteous or the righteousness of God again. Therefore, an effective blood sacrifice for man must be found, however, it must be pure without sin, and it must be the blood of man.

"For because of the offense of one man many be dead, it is necessary by the obedience of one to bring all back to life."

~Romans 5:15

Thus, the plan of salvation was put in place, and from the foundation of the world Jesus died.

Lost Connection With the Father

"Can a woman forget her sucking child, that she should not have compassion on the son of her womb? Yea they may forget, yet will I not forget thee."

~Isaiah 49:15

The disobedience of Adam caused man to lose fellowship with God the Father, and left him empty. He does not know what the emptiness is, but it is evident it is there.

This emptiness manifests itself when men are making large sums of cash, purchase beautiful homes, the finest

A Man Like God

cars, the most beautiful wife, and women and yet is not satisfied. Therefore, he seeks for the fulfillment his soul is missing by doing drugs, employing more sex or more success.

Man believes he will find life's fulfillment in the arms of a woman, the bottom of a bottle, or the end of a pipe. Not to mention the pursuit of knowledge, the endless hours of work, and the constant pursuit of every kind of entertainment.

Men were created to fellowship and communicate with the Lord God; his soul came from God, and longs to be back with the Father. The soul cannot live without the constant connection with the LORD God; thus, he finds something to worship and set his affections on; albeit superficial.

He no longer enjoys God coming to him in the cool of the day to spend time with him. He wonders when he prays does God even hear.

Man is broken and has lost his true identity, his true purpose, and his direction.

Out of the presence of God he is beguiling, unstable, reckless, and foolish. Not understanding or admitting: his soul needs to be reconnected with his Father.

Needs Something More

At some point, we get tired of the many things we purchase or do to bring us joy and fulfillment. After we find out there is really nothing at the bottom of the bottle, the high doesn't last, and sex is too easy. What's left?

IN NEED OF A SAVIOR

This question is pondered by many who've done everything, been everywhere, and still find themselves unfulfilled. We are so busy filling our lives with stuff, and excitement to make us happy not understanding that happiness does not last; joy does.

There is this constant pursuit of more in order to be fulfilled and for life to retain meaning, but the answer is not in more stuff, more activity or more parties; what the soul longs for is more of God.

SALVATION'S PLAN

"The LORD God will raise up unto thee a Prophet from the midst of thee, of thy brethren, like unto me, unto him ye shall hearken."

~Deuteronomy 18:15

Fundamentally, God's plan of salvation in sending Jesus into the earth is a parallel of Adam and Moses.

Just as God created Adam without sin, perfect in his creation, and holy in nature, which Adam forfeited in disobeying God, and was plummeted into a life of Sin and degradation. In this same manner must Jesus come into the world and be placed into the body of man who knew no sin.

The Spirit of God breathed upon Mary (see Luke 1:35) and Jesus became a living soul. However, like Adam, Jesus needed to be tempted with the sin of Satan (see Matthew 4:1), deny him (Satan) as Adam should've done, and to restore the authority, dominion, and rulership back to man through the Father.

Furthermore, in order to keep Satan from assuming power over man again, Jesus would go down into hell

A Man Like God

and preach to those in prison; rise again with the keys of life, death, and the grave. Taking the keys back with him to Heaven; thus severing Satan's authority over the man forever.

Jesus through his life would demonstrate man's power over his flesh, demonstrating authority over Satan and his demons, and would affirm:

"Verily, verily, I say unto you, He that believeth on me, the works that I do shall he do also; and greater works than these shall he do; because I go unto my father."

~John 14:12

Hence, salvation was given to restore, or redeem man back to God, and place him in his former (created) state through Jesus Christ.

Therefore, man if he embraces Jesus Christ as Lord and Savior; is no longer a slave to sin and death, but obtain power over them through Jesus Christ.

Paul recognized this and wrote the following: *"For though I should boast somewhat more of our authority, which the Lord hath given us for edification, and not for your destruction, I should not be ashamed."* 2 Corinthians 10:8

That you might obtain free access to God again without interference of Satan or his minions; God would send His son to die for you and me. His son who did no wrong nor was guile found in him (see 1 Peter 2:22), freely offered his body that you might receive holy boldness to come to the throne of grace.

Not only that, but through Jesus you might renounce sin in the flesh and walk as children of light; understanding you are no longer flesh, but spirit in

IN NEED OF A SAVIOR

Christ Jesus. Jesus first demonstrating the ability to condemn sin in the flesh (see Romans 8:3).

Remember when God referred to the man as also being flesh, He was speaking concerning man's complete embracing of sin. His mind became sinful continually, and could not embrace the spirit of which he is of.

This condition salvation restores.

The Misuse of Salvation

Men we possess such a responsibility in holding up the gift of salvation; to demonstrate it in perfection and true holiness. In this, we've greatly failed.

We've misused our authority, damaged the confidence many placed in us to deliver the true word of God, and to live thereby.

Being saved by the grace of Jesus Christ and obtaining mercy by His grace, we have abused, misused, and raped the Body of Christ.

It is men who have been caught in compromising positions, men who brought down great ministries and men who will not separate themselves from the lust which causes them to misuse the women (and some men) in the congregation.

We claim our salvation with such vigor yet degrade it with our selfishness. Many of us proudly preach the word, but neglect to live out the word. We are as policemen, whose job it is not to abide by the law, but to enforce the law. We, therefore, enforce the commandments of God, but for the most part do not obey the commandments.

A Man Like God

Paul said it this way: *"Thou that sayest a man should not commit adultery, dost thou commit adultery? Thou that abhorrest idols, dost thou commit sacrilege?"*

~Romans 2:22

Men are the catalyst for sexual immorality in the Body of Christ, while we sit in the presence of God and lust, lie, are effeminate, retain open gay relationships, are molesting children, and are lifted in pride in doing so; until we are caught with our hands in the cookie jar.

This, because though we've been redeemed from sin, we still relate to sin; using grace to facilitate our sin. We, who embraced the Lord Jesus as our personal savior, but personify the curse of Adam or nature of Satan.

We place people in positions we know are not personifying Christ. We know about their alternative lifestyles. However, in order to fill a position we think we need in the congregation; we place someone who's not been tried, has not been tested, and has not renounced or turned away from their sin.

Man was given the commandment, man was placed in authority (not woman), and man will give account to God.

It is man whom God placed to be the head in the earth. What excuse will you render to God for not being a true witness of Jesus Christ?

Remember when Achan (see Joshua 6:16:27 and the seventh chapter) touched of the accursed thing and brought it into the camp of Israel? God punished the whole camp and caused them to be defeated before

IN NEED OF A SAVIOR

their enemy AI. In this same manner have men caused God to be angry with the Body of Christ, because we've touched of the accursed thing and profane the name of the Lord by committing whoredom in the midst of the congregation (Body of Christ). However, each shall give in account for their actions.

God Himself shall recon with you because you've not feared to commit fornication, adultery, blasphemy, hypocrisy lust, and murder (if you hate someone you are a murderer) in the congregation of the Lord.

Since Grace has abounded you have made a decision to sin, and say within your heart "God will forgive me." Thus, you have premeditated to commit folly in the Body of Christ.

Men, you've caused the faith of many to waver in God. You've caused many to turn back from God. You've wounded the weak and God shall hold you responsible; unless you repent of your lust and unclean ways.

It shall be so that judgment will begin at the house of God (see 1 Peter 4:17). However, be weary you are not found with the accursed thing in your heart. For there shall nothing which defiles, neither whatsoever works abomination or makes a lie enter into the Kingdom of God (See Revelation 21:27).

God is calling us (men) to take responsibility for our actions and represent Christ in a manner in which he represented himself. "I'm a man" is no longer an excuse to commit such abominations in the Body of Christ. Repent and turn from your pernicious (destructive or deadly) ways.

A Man Like God

SALVATION'S GIFT

> *"But ye shall receive power, after that the Holy Ghost is come upon you: and ye shall be witnesses unto me both in Jerusalem, and in all Judea, and in Samaria, and unto the uttermost part of the earth."*
>
> ~Acts 1:8

The fundamental gift salvation brings is communion with God the Father again. However, there are several benefits salvation gives to man specifically; because man was given the authority, dominion, and power over the Earth. Salvation restores this authority, dominion, and power to the man through Jesus Christ.

However, it also extends power and authority to women. Not over the Earth, but in spiritual matters. The wife rules with her husband in earth, but cannot rule in the earth without a husband. Therefore, she who is unmarried (virgin) is married to the Lord. Women were not created in the image of God, but in the image of a man (see 1 Corinthians 11:8). Also remember Adam was given this dominion before woman was created.

Restored Authority

Man lost his authority, dominion and power to Satan and through the salvation of Jesus Christ man now receives power over his enemy, and is able to subdue him in the name of Jesus Christ.

This means the man is no longer subject to Satan, but Satan is subject to the man through Jesus Christ. As Jesus said: *"Behold, I give unto you power to tread on serpents*

IN NEED OF A SAVIOR

and scorpions (demons), and over all the power of the enemy: and nothing shall by any means hurt you."

~Luke 10:19 with emphasis added

Jesus removed the yoke of Satan off of man's neck and placed a yoke on Satan's neck, and now he must bow to man when he uses the name of Jesus.

However, there are specific things man must do in order for this authority to operate in his life:

1) He must be free of sin (yes, it is possible to live free of sin).

2) He must fast and pray (see Mark 9:29 and Matthew 17:21). (For a better understanding of fasting: see Fasting and The Fasting Edge by Jenstzen Franklin).

3) He must deny himself, pick-up his cross and follow Jesus.

4) He must possess faith (see Hebrews 11:6).

The power and authority which Jesus restored to man is spiritual. Since Satan stole man's spiritual inheritance, it is only fit Jesus restores this spiritual inheritance back to men, for without his spiritual inheritance man cannot communicate with God, the Father.

Power with Jesus

After Jesus had arisen from the dead, he made this statement:

"All power is given unto me in heaven and in earth."

~ Matthew 28:18

A Man Like God

We also receive access to this power for Paul said, *"And (the Father) hath raised us up together, and made us sit together in heavenly places in Christ Jesus."* Ephesians 2:6 emphasis added) *"Herein is our love made perfect, that we may have boldness in the Day of Judgment; because as he is, so are we in this world."*

~1John 4:17

We who are in Christ Jesus are to be exactly as He (Jesus) is; not just as he was. Christ made us one with him even as he and his Father are one.

Not only do we have power over the earth, but Jesus gave us power and authority with him over the world which includes the spirit realm.

However, this power does not operate when we are not at one with the Lord Jesus Christ; for we can do nothing without him (see John 15:5).

Also, those of us in ministry must understand we do not work for Jesus, but with him, as we can't do the work of the Kingdom without the Lord of the Kingdom. We do not possess this power without Jesus.

For this reason we ought to ensure the Lord's presence which comes with the anointing (the power that destroy yokes), is with us before we engage in ministry. Having a degree in theology without the Holy Spirit is counterproductive.

This is why it is imperative that we only do the things in ministry that are sanctioned by the Lord Himself. Building a house of worship, simply because it's fashionable or desired is not a good reason to do so.

IN NEED OF A SAVIOR

Gifts

The power of God is not to be confused with the gifts of God; for the gifts of God are without repentance (see Romans 11:29).

Therefore, one does not need to repent of sin for the gifts which God gives him to operate in his life. However, the power and authority of God, which causes heaven to work in concert with us requires our repentance, submission, and obedience in order for them to be demonstrated in our lives.

Any gift used without repentance is perverted and can be manipulated by demons. As are the gift of prophesy when used in the form of divination, or psychic reading which depend on familiar spirits (demons) to foresee future events.

The gifts of the Spirit are given to be utilized in concert with the Spirit of God, and not to boost one's own pride. They are given to glorify the Lord God, and not to bring glory to one's self.

Be very careful how you use the gifts which are given, because God will not hold them guiltless who misuse His gifts.

"But he knoweth the way that I take: when he hath tried me, I shall come forth as gold." Job 23:10

Chapter 9

MAN RESURRECTED

It's a brand new day which has dawned upon man. He's awakened out of sleep, been revived, restored, and made new. He is no longer dead but made alive through the sacrifice of Jesus Christ.

The death sentence is rescinded; death retains no more dominion over him. Man is now free from sin, free from sickness, and all things which cause to make bound; if we can only believe this.

"If the son therefore shall make you free, ye shall be free indeed."

~John 8:36

To be resurrected means to be brought back from the dead. Anyone who is a slave to sin is dead while they yet live. This means the man who is conceived in sin and shaped in iniquity, though born physically alive; is truly dead.

Therefore, a son born is a son dead until he chooses to believe in the only begotten son of God. *"Jesus said unto her, I am the resurrection, and the life: he that believeth in me, though he were dead, yet shall he live."* John 11:25

Conversely, a man is not complete until he is restored to God again.

Wherefore, true life does not begin until a man is reborn through Jesus Christ by the Holy Ghost.

A Man Like God

ALIVE FROM THE DEAD

"For as in Adam all die,
even so in Christ shall all be made alive."

~1 Corinthians 15:22

Each and every person born under the curse of Adam is born into death. The curse of Adam caused all men to retain a consciousness of sin which by it brings death.

The curse of Adam made all men dead, which is the opposite of the state he was created in being made a living soul. Therefore, Jesus came in the body of a man to die for all men, so they can once again be made alive in him by accepting him as their personal savior.

"I am crucified with Christ: neverthless I live; yet not I, but Christ liveth in me: and the life which I now live in the flesh I live by the faith of the Son of God, who loved me, and gave himself for me."

~Galatians 2:20

Jesus erased the curse of Adam, making us free from death and hell which held us in bondage, and made each of us (who believe and live according to his word) alive again.

Now, though our body dies, we shall never be dead because we believe on the only begotten son of God.

"And whosoever liveth and believeth in me shall never die. Believest thou this?"

~John 11:26

MAN RESURRECTED

Free From Death

The death of Jesus Christ upon the cross made him a curse for us all. So we may not be cursed with the world. This act of him dying in our place, and we receiving him as our Lord and Savior frees us from the law of sin and death.

We, therefore, are not bound by a curse or law of death which the world is bound by. It is, therefore, important we understand the flesh has no part in our service to God. It is simply given so we may interact with our environment, and possess no authority to keep us from the things of God.

Hence it is written: "*God is a Spirit: and they that worship him must worship him in spirit and in truth.*" John 4:24

Paul said elsewhere we should walk in the Spirit and we will not fulfill the lust of the flesh (see Galatians 5:16).

Should we begin again to fulfill the lusts of the flesh, we begin to walk after the flesh and this will bring about death. "*For if ye live after the flesh, ye shall die: but if ye through the Spirit do mortify (destroy) the deeds of the body, ye shall live.*" Romans 8:13

Your body will die, but your soul shall live forever when you make the Lord Jesus Christ, your Lord and Savior.

For this Jesus said: "*It is the spirit that quickeneth; the flesh profiteth nothing: the words that I speak unto you, they are spirit, and they are life.*" John 6:63

A Man Like God

Therefore, the Lord does not deal at all with your flesh which is temporal (temporary). He deals with your soul which is eternal and came from Him. Therefore, your soul will live or die somewhere; better it live forever with Jesus, rather than die forever in hell which was never created for you.

Peasants and Commoners in The Kingdom

A peasant for our benefit is an uncouth, crude, or ill-bred person.

When someone has been cleansed from sin and death by the power of Jesus Christ and begins again to embrace the things he once denied; he is like a peasant in the Kingdom.

Understand we who are born into Christ have been born into a kingdom (see Matthew 4:17), which works differently than a democracy which all of America is under.

In the Kingdom of Heaven, no one can join or move into the Kingdom, they must be born into it making them sons. This is why being a member of a congregation does not save you, or gives you a straight ticket into Heaven. Being faithful to that congregation doesn't give you a free ticket into Heaven; you must be born-again.

Since the world is the Lord's and the fullness thereof, each person who is not born into the Kingdom of Heaven is a commoner. They are not subject to the laws or benefits of the Kingdom, but are kept separate and apart lest they of the Kingdom should learn their ways (see Deuteronomy 20:18 and 2 Corinthians 6:17).

MAN RESURRECTED

When a son of the Kingdom turns and begins to do the things he was cleansed from, he is not thrown out of the Kingdom but is set apart from the company of those who follow fast or hard after God (see 1 Corinthians 5:11).

The peasants (backsliders) then of the Kingdom are those who know the will of the Lord, but continue to follow their own ways engaging in the filth of the world, in the lust of their flesh, and will not be persuaded to turn from those things back to the True and Living God.

However, when they repent they will be restored fully into the Kingdom and immediately partake of the fullness of God.

Commoners are those who are not born of royal blood, as those who are born into the Kingdom are a royal priesthood (see 1 Peter 2:9). They are sinners and were never partakers of this heavenly calling, for which we've, now receive the power to become sons.

Anyone, therefore, who is a backslider has pronounced to themselves death and has rejected the life of Jesus Christ in them-selves. Yet they cease not to be sons, but disobedient children who if they don't repent will be cast out of the Kingdom forever at the judgment of God.

THE UNBELIEF OF BELIEVERS

Though Jesus died for all men, so they might receive life through him, many accepting the gift he has afforded, and embraced the Lord as their personal savior; still embrace the death that sin is.

A Man Like God

Many believers, men and women alike still hold to the idea that because they live in a flesh body, they will always sin in the flesh: holding the notion that no man can live without sinning.

This belief is a lie from the devil to keep one tethered to sin, and, therefore, tethered to death and the curse of Adam.

However, as stated, Jesus through his own death on the cross removed the curse of Adam and sin which doomed all men to death.

> *"For the law of the Spirit of life in Christ Jesus hath made me free from the law of sin and death."*
>
> ~Romans 8:2

The notion we are less than Jesus was, and, therefore, unable to live without the constant mistakes, falling, and sinning has left the Body of Christ weakened and unable to ward off the constant bombardment of temptation from demons to sin.

So we live in a constant state of fear of sinning, and the expectation to sin which causes us to make excuses when we sin. Rather than renouncing sin in all its forms and embrace the truth: Jesus has made us free from sin.

This unbelief in the total power of Jesus Christ to keep us from sin has led again to the lie that we are sinners saved by grace.

Now men, who preach and teach the Word of God, are caught in sins which should not be named among us who call ourselves saints; simply because we've embraced the lust of sin while preaching the law of grace falsely.

MAN RESURRECTED

According to scripture, we are dead to sin having been resurrected from the death of sin, and been made to walk in the newness of life through Jesus Christ (see Romans 6:4).

It is the grace of God who sent His son to die for the world, and His grace which keeps us from obtaining the punishment we rightly deserved.

Grace rests the judgment of God giving man space to repent of their sin, not to allow them to continue in sin.

Unbelief kept us from obtaining the richness of God, because we see ourselves as mere men, and not as sons of God.

"But as many as received him, to them gave he power to become the sons of God, even to them that believe on his name." John 1:12

You are not simply a man, but a Man who's been reborn and resurrected as a son of God, in the image of God with the power to resist sin and temptation in all its forms.

This means that you must embrace all that God through Jesus Christ says you are.

Man holds the key to the earth, and it is man who the devil fights more than any other on this planet.

If you want authority and can't get it lawfully, then you take it by any means necessary. This is what the devil does, and continues to do by keeping men in bondage to who they truly are.

It's the lies of the enemy which convinced men they are sexual beings, who are supposed to bed many women before they settle-down. It is lies which have

A Man Like God

convinced men they cannot live without frequent sexual escapades. It is a lie which says if you don't use it you will lose it.

Furthermore, it is a lie that you cannot live and serve God perfectly. All it takes is for you to deny yourself.

All that men acquaint with being a man is a lie from the devil to distract you from the real man the Lord created you to be.

You are not a man if you do not act as God, for He created you in His image and in his likeness. Therefore, a man is to look like and act like God. Anything less is a lie and an imitation.

AWAKENED FROM SLEEP

"But the natural man receiveth not the things of the Spirit of God: for they are foolishness unto him: neither can he know them, because they are spiritually discerned."
~1 Corinthians 2:14

Anyone who's never received the Lord Jesus as their personal savior is as it were in a deep sleep. They are unable to see the things of God because their mind's eye hasn't been awakened to the truth.

This is why they cannot see the things they do contrary to God's will as wrong. It is the same state many of the Body of Christ is in when they embrace sin again, and is lifted in pride against God. They've fallen back to sleep and cannot see the errors of their ways.

Take a journey with me to the day you first got saved. Do you remember?

MAN RESURRECTED

Do you remember how you couldn't get enough of Jesus? You would talk to him constantly, pray instantly, was in worship service whenever the doors were open, and beat everyone to the prayer service?

Remember how you felt and the question you asked yourself: "Why did I wait so long?"

At that moment, everything you thought you knew about the world and your existence became a lie. The veil of deception was removed, and you saw things in a different way or a new light.

All you wanted was Jesus. Nothing else mattered, you had a new joy, a new outlook on life, and you were happier than you'd ever been before. No one needed to tell you to stop this, or don't do that, because you were all too willing to do whatever the Lord desired of you.

This is the evidence which witnesses you have been awaken out of the sleep of death. This is the fruit of righteousness, and this is the gift of being resurrected through Jesus Christ.

Albeit, many men have fallen back to sleep because they've been deceived to concentrate on their flesh, rather than keep their minds on Jesus, and remain in the spirit. They've bought back into the lie which says men are sexual creatures wrapped up in their loins and unable to control their sexual urges.

Anger, jealousy, and murder are prescribed as the ways of man, but God created him in love, patience, and holiness.

If you've been received into the family of God, but you are still angry, hateful, macho, sexually deviant or

A Man Like God

immoral then you are not the man God created. You are yet asleep for the man whom Jesus died to revive has yet to come forth.

Alive yet Perpetrating Death

"But fornication, and all uncleanness, or covetousness, let it not be once named among you, as becometh saints."

~*Ephesians 5:3*

How is it many profess they are the sons of God, yet live as if they are the seed of Satan? How is it possible to enter the congregation of the Lord and perform as a true child of God, but demonstrate none of His attributes?

How can we who have been chosen to this dispensation embrace the revelry of the world and still proclaim ourselves sons of the Living God?

"Wherefore come out from among them, and be ye separate, saith the Lord, and touch not the unclean thing; and I will receive you."

~2 Corinthians 6:17

"Love not the world, neither the things that are in the world. If any man love the world, the love of the Father is not in him."

~1 John 2:15

Many have fallen asleep and embraced again the dead works which makes one blind to the true things of God. Committing fornication, adultery, and glorifying the world over God.

Why do we embrace the music of this world, the songs which glorify man rather than God, and bring that same music into the congregation of the Lord? How can we say we love God when we eat from the table of the Lord, and turnaround and eat from the tables of demons?

We've been deceived, because we thought to bring in the entertainment of the world to draw the world, when all we've done is draw demons into the congregation of the Lord. You cannot transform the world using the world's devices.

We profess we know the Lord, but in action we deny Him. Many worshipping with their lips, but their heart is far from Him. We've learned behaviors in the congregation and called it Holy, bringing in the dance of the world and playing before the Lord.

So-called men of God lay their hands on us, and we've learned how to pretend we are falling under the power of God. We've learned how to imitate the power in order not to receive the true power of God. In our homes, we have learned the dance steps to play before the Lord, but not to live Holy in the presence of God.

Men have placed themselves over the Children of God and played the whore with abominations, abusing themselves with men in the congregation of the Lord, and enter the Holy place as if they did nothing wrong.

We say we are alive and yet we live as the dead? Men's loins become their gods while making excuses for not taking responsibility for the mess made with their loins.

God comes to reckon with you, for you have lifted yourself in fleshly pride: using His offices for your own

A Man Like God

pleasures, ruling over His people with rigor, and commanding them to obey your words more than the word of God.

You've become rich on the backs of His people, living delicately while you spoil them as men who divide the prey, and keep them in bondage to a dead system. You've levied their lives for gain and caused them to blaspheme His name.

"These are spots in your feasts of charity, when they feast with you, feeding themselves without fear; clouds they are without water, carried about of winds; trees whose fruit withereth, without fruit, twice dead, plucked up by the roots; raging waves of the sea, foaming out their own shame; wandering stars, to whom is reserved the blackness of darkness forever."

~Jude 1:12-13

It is time for men to change their ways, and embrace God in His fullness. Repent of every evil way and return to the Lord and He will return to you.

Chapter 10

THE MAN: JESUS

One of the greatest pictures of a man like God is Jesus Christ, who was God.

"Who being in the form of God, thought it not robbery to be equal with God: but made himself of no reputation, and took upon him the form of a servant, and was made in the likeness of men: And being found in fashion as a man, he humbled himself, and became obedient unto death, even the death of the cross."

~Philippians 2:6-8

Jesus was flesh and blood, and endured the same temptations we do. He had the same pressures, the same battles growing up, and endured all the things men go through in this life:

"For we have not an high priest which cannot be touched with the feeling of our infirmities; but was in all points tempted like as we are, yet without sin."

~Hebrews 4:15

Many men believe that because Jesus was the son of God somehow this exempted him from experiencing all the oppression of the enemy to commit sin. Also, this is the same excuse they use not to meet the mark Jesus himself set.

If this were true it would exempt Jesus from being able to die for us, or take our place on the Cross. He needed to be tempted, tried, oppressed, and suppressed

A Man Like God

by all we go through in order to redeem us back to God.

The only thing one could say separates us from Jesus, is he had the complete knowledge of the spirit realm, which we who've never been outside the body possess. Yet Jesus had to come as one of us in order to destroy the curse of Adam, which was in us. He must go through everything we endure as "humans" in order to be a suitable sacrifice for us.

In this same why has Jesus sent us the Holy Ghost, the same spirit which was in him and raised him from the dead, which can give us the knowledge of the spirit realm with the conversations of Heaven.

"Howbeit when he, the Spirit of truth, is come, he will guide you into all truth: for he shall not speak of himself; but whatsoever he shall hear, that shall he speak: and he will shew you things to come."

~John 16:13

Therefore, being equipped with everything Jesus possesses, we can now do everything Jesus did and more.

For three years Jesus walked in Jerusalem preaching, teaching and demonstrating all we would be able to do through him in the person of the Holy Ghost.

He did not come to operate above us, but to be the forerunner of that which the Apostles would later demonstrate in fullness after Jesus ascended on high. Therefore, we should not look upon Jesus' life and think we can't do what he did, when he has expressively told us to do so.

THE MAN: JESUS

So when we say we can't do such and such because we are not Jesus or God, we are making excuses to continue in the things contrary to God.

AS HE IS SO ARE WE

"Herein is our love made perfect, that we may have boldness in the Day of Judgment: because as he is, so are we in this world."

~1 John 4:17

Men go through much length to stay in a low estate in Christ, when Jesus made it possible for us to reach the highest heights in him. We constantly degrade ourselves to be less than Christ when he himself said:

"It is enough for the disciple that he be as his master, and the servant as his lord. If they have called the master of the house Beelzebub, how much more shall they call them of his household?"

~Matthew 10:25

To be like something or someone, is to be similar in appearance, or behave in the same manner as another. In this case, Jesus is saying it is enough for the servant to be as his master, as in displaying His mannerisms.

So, each of us is to have the same look and the same mannerisms as Jesus, obtaining the same likes, dislikes, and hatred of.

Now Jesus is our example of what we as sons of God (Men) should be and how we should operate in this life. He is the new image of God. Jesus is as we should be.

Scripture states, as he (Jesus) is, so, are we in this world (see 1 John 4:17). So why is it so hard for us who

A Man Like God

have received the gift of the Holy Ghost, to believe we are everything Jesus was and is?

Who is Jesus? Jesus was God in the flesh according to the scripture:

"In the beginning was the Word, and the Word was with God, and the Word was God. And the Word was made flesh, and dwelt among us, (and we beheld his glory, the glory as of the only begotten of the father,) full of grace and truth."

~John 1:1, 14

We see the Word of God was made flesh in the person of Jesus Christ, which makes Jesus God because the scripture states; the Word was God. We then as children of the Most High God are to become the Word of God through much study:

"Study to shew thyself approved unto God, a workman that needeth not to be ashamed, rightly dividing the word of truth."

~2 Timothy 2:1

This means the word of God (the Bible) is not to remain words on a page, but is to become a part of who we are; just as we are not to have church, but be the temples of God, to be the Church. In other words, we are to do exactly what the word says, which means we must be one with the Word of God, or the Word of God must become us.

There should be no separation between men and the Word of God. In this manner, we become as Jesus is. With this the excuse: "There is only one perfect man and its Jesus" is no longer valid. For Jesus said: *"Be ye therefore perfect, even as your father who is in Heaven is perfect."* Matthew 5:48

THE MAN: JESUS

Remember Adam was a perfect man, created in the image and likeness of God. It wasn't until he disobeyed God that imperfection (sin) was introduced to men.

We, therefore, who have been born into this dispensation and received the gift of the Holy Ghost are made again perfect before God through Jesus Christ. We are as he is.

It is, therefore, impossible for anyone to be like Christ, or personify Christ and not possess the Holy Ghost:

"But ye are not in the flesh, but in the Spirit, if so be that the Spirit of God dwell in you. Now if any man have not the Spirit of Christ, he is none of his."

~Romans 8:9

So whether you believe in the indwelling of the Holy Ghost or not, scripture states, if you do not have the Holy Ghost you are none of his (God's). Which means, you cannot personify Christ; you cannot be perfect without that which is perfect: The Holy ghost.

Therefore, say not: "I am not Jesus", but profess Christ the hope of Glory lives in you:

"Let this mind be in you, which was also in Christ Jesus."

~Philippians 2:5

Remembering that the servant will never be greater than his lord or master, but he can be as, or like his master.

A Man Like God

We are As He Is: Powerful

"But ye shall receive power, after that the Holy Ghost is come upon you: and ye shall be witnesses unto me both in Jerusalem, and in all Judaea, and in Samaria, and unto the uttermost part of the earth."

~Acts 1:8

Though man has been given all authority, and power to use that authority, he still feels fundamentally powerless. Mainly because he attempts to use his power in a system which he is no longer a part of. We are in this world but not of this world.

Jesus has given to us all the power we need to control, and transform kingdoms in this earth.

"And Jesus came and spake unto them, saying, All power is given unto me in heaven and in earth."

~Matthew 28:18

No one will dispute the fact that Jesus received all power, he is all powerful, and there is nothing impossible to him. However, many hardly believe he (Jesus) has given us access to that power as well, but Jesus testified this to his disciples:

"Behold, I give unto you power to tread on serpents and scorpions, and over all the power of the enemy: and nothing shall by any means hurt you."

~Luke 10:19

Is this not the epitome of power? Power is the ability to act or produce an effect; therefore, Jesus gave us the power to act upon his word, and to witness his word

THE MAN: JESUS

producing an effect. Not only so, but because it is witnessed in scripture:

"*Thou shalt also decree a thing, and it shall be established unto thee: and the light shall shine upon thy ways.*"

~Job 22:28

The words you speak in accordance to his word will also be established. This power is not for a select few (those who place a title on their name and expect others to come to them for something from God), but God's given every man who receives him as Lord and is willing and obedient; power.

This power is not only to heal the sick, raise the dead, or cast out demons (see Mark 16:17), but also we will be able to deny the fleshly desires of our bodies, and serve God in peace of mind:

"*Thou wilt keep him in perfect peace, whose mind is stayed on thee: because he trusteth in thee.*"

~Isaiah 26:3

The power Jesus gives to us is all inclusive. Meaning nothing is impossible if we only believe (see Mark 9:23).

In that Jesus gives us power over serpents and scorpions, he also gives us power over kingdoms: Both spiritual and natural, so that through the Spirit of God, we could call those things which be not as though they were.

Wherefore, many men will say they can't come to God because they can't go without sex. Conversely, many men say they can't live right because they need sex. In this they deny the power of God within themselves, and chose rather to enjoy the pleasure of sin for a season, rather than surrender to the authority of Jesus Christ, which will make them whole.

Any man who thinks the abundance of his ability to be male comes from his loins is in error. We've already concluded man is man even without a body. Therefore, if a man loses the activity of his penis, this does not sever his ability to be a man. For he is not a man simply because he owns a penis, engages in frequent sex with women, or can produce children.

Therefore, it is very possible for a man to live in Christ and not engage in sexual immorality or perversions. The power to resist one's own sexual urge is called control. If a man does not have the ability to control his own desires, he is unruly and devilish.

Many in the Body of Christ possess a form of godliness but constantly deny the power thereof. Each time we say: "I can't" we deny the power, when we say, "its impossible" we also deny the power.

When we agree with the doctor who tells us a disease is incurable, we deny the power. When we affirm that we will always sin, we deny the power God's given us to live holy in this world. To live Holy means to live without sin.

Love

Many men fall way short on this one. Many love as long as they can get something from it, someone does what they want, or they can manipulate the other person. This is not the love of Christ.

THE MAN: JESUS

Christ loves unconditionally; he required nothing of us before he died nothing before he healed; except our faith.

We as sons of God are to personify love not only receive love. We are to exude love and to exist in love. Jesus commanded us to love one another even as he loves us (see John 13:354).

Remember we are as he is, at least we should be. This means that in the same way Jesus loves us, we should love one another. Whether they are our enemy or our friend we are instructed to love (see Luke 6:27), and in love forgive.

Love does not wait ıfor someone to ask for forgiveness, as Jesus did not wait for us to ask forgiveness of our sins before he died, but we should be swift to forgive, because if we don't forgive, our Heavenly Father will not forgive us.

Without faith, it is impossible to please God and faith works by love (see Hebrews 11:6 and Galatians 5:6). Love does no ill or wrong to his brother even when the brother does wrong to you.

The world's love is conditional; we are instructed to have unconditional love, to love regardless of ill will, or harm.

The Love of God is what keeps us in the will of God. It is written this way:

"For this is the love of God, that we keep his commandments: and his commandments are not grievous."

~1 John 5:3

A Man Like God

For one to say he loves God, but does not do the things which God commands him to do, is to be a liar (see 1 John 2:4). Therefore how can we say we love the Lord, but engage in all manner of lust and deviant behavior, and unforgiveness?

Someone talking about you, lying on you, casting your name out as evil, destroying your property, or wounding your flesh are not reasons to forsake love. In fact, these are the very ways in which Jesus has told us to love.

"But I say unto you which hear, Love your enemies, do good to them which hate you, bless them that curse you, and pray for them which despitefully use you."

~Luke 6:27-28

Therefore, there's been a lie told that men are to have difficulty with expressing love, or be afraid of commitment. It is a lie the enemy has devised to keep men in hate, and animosity, hating and killing one another in the name of reputation, or the fear of appearing weak.

The enemy has deceived men in thinking we have to be a playa, to enjoy sex with many women and call it love. Love is not sex, is not manipulative, and is not selfish or self-willed. Love does not seek its own pleasure, or oppress others for its own desires, but nurtures and cares for all especially those of its own (see 1 Corinthians 13).

Love is what caused God to created man in the first place. Therefore, if you do not, or cannot love, you are not of God.

THE MAN: JESUS

Anti-Christ

Anti-Christ means to be against Jesus Christ: Therefore, if you perform any of the sins the Lord has commanded us to stay away from, you are an antichrist. If you teach lies as truth you are an antichrist, if you hate your brother with or without a cause; you are a murderer and an antichrist.

Wherefore, let us love one another in Spirit and in truth, as the Lord requires each of his children to do.

CORNERSTONE OF THE CHURCH

"Now therefore ye are no more strangers and foreigners, but fellowcitizens with the saints, and of the household of God; And are built upon the foundation of the apostles and prophets, Jesus Christ himself being the chief corner stone."
~Ephesians 2:19-20

Jesus who having suffered, bled, and died; rose again on the third day, received all power in Heaven and in earth, has risen to be the only head of his body the Church.

Therefore, there is no one else on earth that can possess a church, for no other man upon the face of the earth died for a people like Jesus did.

What we call the church is simply a building we've purchased, leased or rented, and not the true Chruch of the Lord Jesus Christ.

The church of God is not a building made with brick and mortar, but a building of flesh and spirit in that the body carries the spirit of the Living God (the Holy Ghost) within it.

A Man Like God

You then individually become the temple of the Living God, and collectively the Church of Jesus Christ; a living host for a Living God.

As stated in a previous chapter, if you view the building as the Church, more than you view your own body as the Church or temple of God; you will honor the building more than the true temple of God; you.

This is why it is so easy for us to stray away from the Word of God, because we don't see ourselves as the temples of God, we who carry the Spirit of God within us wherever we go as the priest carried the Ark of God in the wilderness.

So the next time you are tempted to engage, demean, or debase yourself to sin; remember the Holy Ghost is there with you, and reporting all you do back to the Judge of all the Earth.

Sin destroys the temple (body), and whosoever destroys the temple; **him shall God destroy**.

Chapter 11

AUTHORITY WITH CHRIST

Man's become so weak in his representation of Jesus Christ, in that he no longer represents Christ in a manner to which He represented himself. Furthermore, many of us don't represent the Apostles or do them the service they are befitting of.

We carry the authority of Christ in word only, but the power to utilize that authority is all but null and void.

We pronounce many words to say what Jesus can do, but possess not the power and authority to perform perfectly what He does. We are weak and yet we say we are strong, we've become delusional yet profess we are wise in the things of Christ.

Yet the Body of Christ dies within while hearing the words of the Kingdom in our worship services on Sunday, in the prayer meetings, and Bible studies; while sitting in the midst of the congregation of the Lord unable to break free of the simplest bondages.

We profess we know Christ while in sickness many deny him, while many pastors send saints to psychologist and psychiatrist instead of casting out a demon. Our God is a spirit, but we attempt to utilize natural methods to rid ourselves of spiritual problems.

We want the power, but we don't want to deny ourselves anything to obtain that power. We desire

A Man Like God

authority but won't sacrifice ourselves for authority. The price was paid to afford us this authority, but we don't want to pay the price to utilize that same authority.

We've become a people of talk with little action. No wonder the world looks upon us and wags their head, or mock us to our faces.

Is it any wonder why we are transformed by governments instead of governments being transformed by us, the so-called children of the Most High God?

However, the power and authority of God will be demonstrated, but where will you stand when they are?

Working With The Lord

"And they went forth, and preached everywhere, the Lord working with them, and confirming the word with signs following. Amen."

~Mark 16:20

The first things we must understand in utilizing the authority of Christ is that we must work with the Lord, not for him.

When we work for someone, they don't have to be there in order for us to complete our duties, however, when we work with someone, we can't start working until they show up. This signified by scripture:

*"I am the vine, ye are the branches; He that abideth in me, and I in him, the same bringeth forth much fruit: **for without me ye can do nothing**."*

~John 15:51

AUTHORITY WITH CHRIST

Therefore, when we attempt to do service unto the Lord, and do that service without the Lord's presence, or we devise things to do and attach the Lord to it; we are not working with the Lord. In this manner, the authority of God and the power to utilize that authority does not accompany us in what we say we are doing for the Lord.

This is why we can go days, weeks, months, and years without the demonstration of the power of God, because we have begun to trust in our gifting's rather than the presence of Jesus Christ. We do not wait on his presence, and go about trusting in the work instead of the God of the work.

We have elevated our gifts, so that now we encourage people to come see us in our giftings, but do not encourage the saints to seek God's presence. Our titles have become more important than God's presence, and the pride of many have reduced our worship services to talent shows.

If the time you spend in your worship services is more important than the healing of God's people you are not working with the Lord. In other words, if the Lord does not have free course to extend your worship service, then you are in service for yourself, not with the Lord.

Assignment

In order for the authority of Jesus Christ to operate in our lives, we must first receive an assignment from the Lord and operate in the confines of that assignment. To deviate from that assignment is to be out of the will of the Lord.

A Man Like God

Within our assignments, the Lord must accompany us; in other words, work with us in fulfilling his will because as stated before "we can do nothing without Him."

The assignment of the Lord is not about you, your gift, or you're anointing, but the purpose of the Lord entirely, and may not include you having your own congregation.

Therefore, the assignment of the Lord has nothing to do with your desires, and is not a career move. It is given to advance the Kingdom of Heaven alone.

You then become a utensil in the purpose of God, and must be willing and obedient to be utilized in this fashion. In this manner, it doesn't matter who does prayer on Sunday, as long as it is someone whom the Lord has assigned, and not someone chosen based on friendship.

When you understand that you are a utensil on assignment from the Lord, you do not get hung-up on personalities, positions, or who always does a certain thing. You are only concerned with the assignment the Lord has given you, and completing that assignment.

"Jesus saith unto them, My meat (assignment) is to do the will of him that sent me, and to finish his work."

~John 4:34

Jesus understood that while he was in the earth his duty was to finish the work (assignment) the Father gave him. The assignment was not to bring glory to himself, or bring honor to himself, but to the Father.

AUTHORITY WITH CHRIST

If the only begotten son of God can understand His assignment, why can't we understand ours?

The authority and power of God, which causes the Host of Heaven to assist us in all that we do; operates only with those who have been given an assignment from the Lord.

Assignments are different than signs, for the signs of God (raising the dead, healing the sick, and casting out demons) are for anyone who will believe, but the assignments of God are given to specific people, for a specific purpose at a specific time or span of time.

Noah was assigned to build an Ark, Moses was given an assignment to lead the children of Israel out of Egypt, Joshua was given an assignment to lead the children of Israel over Jordan to possess the land of promise, and distribute their inheritance. David was assigned king over Israel, John the Baptist was assigned the forerunner of Jesus, Jesus was assigned to redeem the world, and Paul was assigned to Apostle the gentiles.

Assignments are not gifts or signs which all are partakers of, but assignments are specific tasks which the Lord himself assigns to whomsoever He desires, and to whom much is given, of him shall much be required (see Luke 12:48).

Provisions for the Assignment

With every assignment which the Lord has assigned he provides the provisions for it. He makes a way, and he alone supplies the needs for that assignment. Whether it is touching the hearts of men to support or

A Man Like God

providing supernaturally, all provision are made by the Lord and should be expected from the Lord.

One should never burden people with an assignment they say God gave them, for if God give it He will make provisions for it, and supply the help to establish what He has set forth.

If someone is begging or pleading with the congregation to help support an assignment they said God gave them, then perhaps God didn't give it, or maybe they have stepped out of timing. For God is very well able to support what He has ordained.

Therefore, for those who have started ministries, or congregations, and have begun to demand specific amounts, or commanded the people of God to give a certain amount each week, or month; you are out of order.

"But this I say, He which soweth sparingly shall reap also sparingly; and he which soweth bountifully shall reap also bountifully. **Every man according as he purposes in his heart***, so let him give; not grudgingly, or of necessity: for God loveth a cheerful giver."*

~2 Corinthians 9:6:-7

When God assigns help to an assignment He's instituted, it is based on their free will, not on the demand. Hence, when God instructed the people to bring an offering for the building of the Tabernacle in the Wilderness, He said, *"everyone who is of a willing heart* (see Exodus 35:5)." God Himself made no demands of the people to give large or small, but left it up to them how much they wanted to give.

AUTHORITY WITH CHRIST

When you cause the people of God to give grudgingly, or of necessity, you cause them to lose the benefits they would receive from God because they don't give of a willing heart. Also, causing them to give out of fear is not the will of God.

If God through Jesus has given you an assignment, then trust Him to supply all your needs according to His riches in Glory.

SPIRITUAL AUTHORITY

"Behold, I give unto you power to tread on serpents, and scorpions, and over all the power of the enemy: and nothing shall by any means hurt you."
~Luke 10:19

The most underused, or misused authority in the Kingdom of Heaven is spiritual authority.

Spiritual authority is given to each temple of the Body of Christ; everyone filled with the gift of the Holy Ghost is given spiritual authority. It is not something one earns, but is a birthright of everyone born into the Kingdom.

This authority works with the gifts of the Spirit to demonstrate the power of God to subdue kingdoms and authorities, such as demonic authority and diabolical kingdoms.

It is given to subdue everything which would war against the furtherance of the Kingdom of Heaven; to destroy infirmities, the oppression and depression of demons, and Satan.

A Man Like God

In order then to utilize this spiritual authority, one must understand spiritual matters, spiritual warfare, and their position in the Kingdom; which the Body of Christ is deficient in.

Understanding Spiritual Matters

"For we wrestle not against flesh and blood, but against principalities, against powers, against the rulers of the darkness of this world, and against spiritual wickedness in high places."

~Ephesians 6:12

If the above is true (and it is), why then do we spend so much time wrestling against one another, fighting for positions, titles, or our day on the pulpit?

How is it so easy to demean one another, and cast each other down simply because we don't like what the other says, or does?

The answer is because we are blind to the inner workings of demon spirits, which causes havoc and spurn divisions. We believe because we are saved, or filled with the Holy Ghost, demons can't use us for evil. Yet he is pitting brothers against one another every day.

We can't see this and began to bicker and fight one with another instead of rising up against demon spirits whose job it is to divide and conquer.

Wherefore, because we are blind and truly are ignorant of the devil's devices, we spend our time dividing ourselves, rather than uniting against our true enemy.

The other reason we can't see demons working behind the scenes is because we carry too much fault

AUTHORITY WITH CHRIST

against one another which blinds us to the truth of what is really happening.

Therefore, if you are going to understand or gain insight into the spiritual world, you must put away all animosity against any and all persons, dead or alive.

You must further possess the ability to learn a person not only by their flesh, but also by spirit. You must pray frequently and interact with Jesus Christ constantly in order to get to know him, and the spirit of God; because once you know who Jesus is, you know who and what He is not.

The Word of God must be adhered to in its entirety. The Word of God gives insight to the enemy; insight which you can use to defeat demons. You must also know yourself, your desires, your short-comings, and what you desire of the Lord.

These things help in discerning when the enemy is attacking you, and when it is your own will and emotions taking over.

You must acknowledge that everything done in this world is influenced by either demon spirits or by the Spirit of God. To believe man is alone, and operates in and of himself, is to be doomed to the devices of the enemy.

We must learn the fruits of the enemy and the fruits of the Spirit, in order to understand when something is being directed by God, or by demons.

Your personal feelings must be brought under the authority of Jesus Christ in order not to take personal those things, or people the enemy is using against you.

A Man Like God

"Let all bitterness, and wrath, and anger, and clamour (a loud persistent outcry), and evil speaking, be put away from you, with all malice (a desire to inflict injury): And be ye kind one to another, tenderhearted, forgiving one another, even as God for Christ's sake hath forgiven you."

~Ephesians 4:31-32

Wherefore, because we did not understand the workings of demons, many congregations, and ministries have been dissolved, because many fought against each other, instead of recognizing the operations of demons.

In order to truly gain an understanding of spiritual matters, we must gain control of ourselves. If we are unruly in our own spirits, how can we control the spirits of demons who uses our feelings, emotions, and desires against us?

Remember, you are not flesh but spirit. Why then do you only concentrate on the natural?

The Tongue

"Death and life are in the power of the tongue: and they that love it shall eat the fruit thereof."
~Proverbs 18:21

The tongue has the potential to be utilized for good or for evil. It possesses the power to heal and to wound, to cause life, or to take life away.

In the Kingdom of God, the tongue is to be utilized at all times as an instrument of life and health. *"Bless them which persecute you: bless, and curse not."* Romans 12:14

AUTHORITY WITH CHRIST

The authority which the tongue gives us is to decree the word of God in the earth, and decree them established (see Job 22:28). However, the tongue only speaks that which is in the heart:

"O generations of vipers, how can ye, being evil, speak good things? For out of the abundance of the heart the mouth speaketh."

~Matthew 12:34

It is, therefore, important the Word of God is embedded in the heart in order for the Word of God to be extracted out of it. The tongue can be a powerful weapon for the Lord if it is ordered aright. For the authority of the Kingdom are enforced through God's Word spoken in due season.

Double Tongue

A double or forked tongue is like a double-minded man; unstable. One cannot be divided in thought or action when utilizing the authority of Jesus Christ.

One who would bless God in one sentence and curse their neighbor in the next is not fitted for the Kingdom of God. If you possess the capacity to speak ill of someone when you are angry, then you are not fully delivered in your heart.

Sweet and bitter water cannot come from the same fountain, nor does a tree bear both good and bad fruit. Therefore, the son of God must stand on sure ground one way or another.

The Lord will not be as understanding to sin as many believe, but will cast both it and them in outer

A Man Like God

darkness. It is, therefore, expedient we be sure on whose side we are on.

You cannot bless and curse, you cannot be saint and sinner, and you cannot serve the Lord and Satan at the same time.

Remember what the Lord said:

"Many will say to me in that day, Lord, Lord, have we not prophesied in they name? and in thy name have cast out devils? And in they name done many wonderful works? And then will I profess unto them, I never knew you: depart from me, ye that work iniquity."

~Matthew 7:22-23

Therefore, be sure whose side you are standing on when you open your mouth.

Chapter 12

THE MAN LIKE GOD

Jesus has walked the path we as men in Christ should walk. In the same manner in which he operated is the manner to which he expects us to operate. The same love he expressed without expecting anything in return is the way he expects us to express his love.

Men if redeemed by Jesus Christ should be merciful, gentle, easily to be entreated, and quick to love. If he's truly made of the same things existent in God the Father, then it should be clearly seen by those around him.

The Lord expects you to be everything He is. No excuse will free you from the responsibilities of being a son of God created in the image and likeness of God, who Jesus has redeemed again to God.

No Excuses

"All things are lawful unto me, but all things are not expedient: all things are lawful for me, but all things edify not."

~1 Corinthians 10:23

Many are filled with excuses or reasons they can't do the things requested of them; none which are based on the truth of the Gospel, but lies perpetrated by demon spirits.

"I can't," is a lie from the enemy, which is usually followed by something the Lord commanded us to do.

A Man Like God

"I can't stand him or her" as opposed to I love him or her as instructed by the Lord. Even if they have made themselves your enemy you are instructed to love them.

"I can't go without sex" when the Lord has commanded us to abstain from fornication and adultery.

Wherefore, we allow lies to be a part of who we are in order to continue living below the standard set by Jesus Christ. Who also said:

"All things are possible to them that believe."

~Mark 9:23

It is much easier to give into our own personal lusts, idiosyncrasies (A structural or behavioral characteristic peculiar to an individual or group), and selfishness rather than deny ourselves and do as Christ has done.

Man has perfected the ability to do wrong and make excuses for the wrong he does. On the other hand, many embrace the wrong they've done, only to appear to people more righteous than they actually are.

There will be no excuse you could render to the Lord for your denial to do what he commanded. "I'm not perfect" will not be accepted when you come face to face with yourself before the Lord Jesus.

BORN OF TRUTH

"Only fear the LORD, and serve him in truth with all your heart: for consider how great things he hath done for you."
~1 Samuel 12:24

Every man born of the Spirit of God (Holy Ghost) is born of truth, for the Spirit of God is truth (see John 16:13). Man, therefore, is to walk in truth, establish

THE MAN LIKE GOD

truth, and demonstrate truth in all he does before the Lord.

There is no room for him to engage in falsehoods and lies. Therefore, for men to even be acquainted with anything false or which makes a lie is against his true nature. We are not to be partakers of theft (purchasing bootleg videos, music, software or anything which has been created by stealing from the original designer), lies, or anything contrary to sound doctrine.

Our God is a God of truth, justice, and love, we as representatives of Him should operate in the same manner, as not to cause others to blaspheme His Holy name.

CANNOT SIN

"Whosoever is born of God doth not commit sin; for his seed remaineth in him: and he cannot sin, because he is born of God."

~1 John 3:9

We must change our mentality in order to stop the enclave of men who live below the standard of Holiness, and engage in all manner of sinful pleasures, and deny the Lord Jesus, who redeemed them from the curse of sin and death.

Man has been redeemed from sin and redeemed to God, who knew no sin. It is, therefore, required that men not engage in any sin while naming the Lord Jesus Christ as his Lord and savior.

When man engages in the sin he's been redeemed from, he walks in the spirit of lies which seeks to keep him tethered to sin and death.

A Man Like God

He is in Christ, therefore, can never die, but he perpetrates death (sin) which will cause him to die again eternally.

When scripture says whosoever is born of God cannot sin, He is making a decree that man born of His Spirit will never sin because he is no longer conceived in sin and shaped in iniquity. Man is now born of the same spirit which God is of, and as God cannot sin, neither can they who are born of Him sin.

This takes great faith by the man born of God because he has to stop thinking of himself, as a male in the flesh, and see himself as a Man in Spirit, born by Spirit, and living of the Spirit of God, which knows no sin.

If you are convinced that you will never be able to live sinless in the flesh; then you have been convinced by the lies of demons to continue in sin.

"God forbid. How shall we, that are dead to sin, live any longer therein?"

~Romans 6:2

Understand all men have sinned, but in and through Jesus Christ we no longer are slaves to sin, sin possess no dominion over us (see Romans 6:9). We have been made free of sin and, therefore, are not slaves to sin in the flesh for we are not flesh.

"But ye are not in the flesh, but in the Spirit, if so be that the Spirit of God dwell in you. Now if any man have not the Spirit of Christ, he is none of his."

~Romans 8:9

THE MAN LIKE GOD

Capacity to Sin

Having the ability or capacity to sin does not mean we should sin. Though we remember the days of sin, and still have the same desires within use to fulfill the lust which once worked within us without conviction, we should constantly seek to do away with the nature of sin in the flesh.

Many may have a desire to live without committing the sin of the flesh, but find themselves back in the very things they promised they would not touch again. Paul was in this same dilemma and made the following statement:

"I find then a law, that, when I would do good, evil is present with me."

~Romans 7:21

For this reason in another place, he said:

"For we wrestle not against flesh and blood, but against principalities, against powers, against the rulers of the darkness of this world, against spiritual wickedness in high places."

~Ephesians 6:12

Therefore, the issue is not the desires of the flesh, but the enemy who constantly manipulate the desires of the flesh, to keep you catering to the flesh.

When the enemy attacks your flesh with sexual desires, he not only attacks your loins, but also your mind and emotions; reminding you how your flesh feels when you engaged in these unlawful deeds. This is why it often seems difficult to escape the lusts of the flesh,

A Man Like God

because it feels so good, and we just want to feel good, Right?

For this reason did Jesus give us power over all the works of the enemy (see Luke 10:19), so we would not be slaves to obey our own lust; which the enemy manipulates and causes us to fall prey to.

Any habit or desire you can't control (for the Lord has given us control) is the inner working of demon spirits oppressing you to continue in the lustful pleasures of the flesh.

Bad language is lust of the flesh, fornication, anger, wrath, murder (the same is hatred), sedition, heresies, and all such are also fruits of the devil.

As sons of God, we should not be producing fruits of demons, but beloved fruits of our Lord and Savior Jesus Christ.

Your ability to renounce sin in the flesh will first stem from your belief (faith) in the ability of God in man to do so, with the assistance of the Lord Jesus.

However, If you will not believe it is possible, then you will never experience it, and continue to fall prey to the sins which you have been delivered of.

You defeat the purpose of salvation within you when you don't believe all is possible through Jesus Christ, or he has the power to keep you from sin; for whatsoever is not done of faith is sin (see Romans 14:23).

It is time for men to turn the tides of what is expected of us as becomes saints, or sons of God. We must begin to renounce sin in the flesh and take a stand

THE MAN LIKE GOD

for true Holiness while also holding each other responsible for the image of Christ we portray.

We must stop celebrating the error of man and establishing our own righteousness, making ourselves appear more righteous than we truly are; engaging in all manner of deviant behavior, and lifting ourselves in pride in that behavior, because we are men.

Being men does not give us the right to dishonor our bodies, or that of the women we relate to. Being men does not give us the right to plant our loins in any woman (or man) we deem accessible at the time. It is not a license to behave in a manner unbefitting of Him who created us; especially if we name Him the Lord of our lives.

Young man, old man, stand up and take your place as the head in the earth, and represent God in whose image you were formed, and whose likeness you were shaped. Live up to the standards of which Christ redeemed you to, and let the world know the sons of God has returned.

We will be in presence, in demeanor, and in reputation men; created again Man.

FREELY EXPRESSES LOVE

"Jesus said unto him, Thou shalt love the Lord thy God with all thy heart, and with all thy soul, and with all thy mind."

~Matthew 22:37

Why should it seem a hard thing for men to freely express love, when he is created by a God of love who is love?

A Man Like God

Men are viewed as possessing a keen disregard or opposition to love. It's far easier to simply have sex with multiple partners than to commit to one wife, and love her with all the heart, and give himself for her as Christ also gave Himself for the church.

Unfortunately, men stumble into love, clumsily, sometimes even pathetically; when he should simply walk into love with his eyes wide open. Freely giving love with all his being. He is created, built, and designed to love.

Love is man's true nature; you see it in the heart of every man-child born. His first instinct is to love, care for, guard, protect, secure, and nurture until he is taught to be angry, hate, murder, to be abusive, self-serving, and malicious.

The devil has oppressed men into believing he is strong, and wise when he express hate, or anger without restraint.

There's a sense of pride in being able to subdue another man or women with senseless anger and hatred. However, scripture says a fool's wrath is presently known (see Proverbs 12:16).

The Love of God demonstrated by a man like God is pure, gentle, easily dealt with, long-suffering, gentle, kind, never proud, and does not boast itself in matters too high for him.

1 Corinthians chapter 13 expresses the heart of God greatly and demonstrates the love men should have both for one another and their female counterparts.

The Man Like God

You young and old man were not created to kill, belittle, demean, bemoan, oppress, and kill one another, but to love one another as you love yourself.

You are not strong, but weak when you can fight before you think, when you can't take someone speaking a word out of turn to you without wanting to do them bodily harm.

The devil has lied to you, he is destroying you. War is not the nature of man; love is, for he has been created in the image and likeness of God, who created man in love (albeit war is sometimes necessary in this world).

God created you in love; therefore, you are wanted, craved, desired, and needed by God. You are God's heart, the apple of His eye.

Your true nature is not to retaliate when someone does you wrong, but to love them in spite of them, to forgive them when they seem unforgivable, and to freely love them when they seemingly are unlovable.

You are a man like God, and you express God's heart in all you do. You are not a second-class citizen, or a haphazard thought. You are an intention and extension of God, set to be the head, not the tail, and established as lord in the earth. Stand in your rightful position and decree your place in God.

Faithful

"A faithful man shall abound with blessings: but he that maketh haste to be rich shall not be innocent."

Proverbs 20:28

A Man Like God

When a man is faithful to God, there will be no issue with him being faithful to his fellow man.

God requires men to be faithful in all he does, be it business, marriage, home, family, or friend. However, it is most important that the man be faithful to God.

We measure faithfulness by how much the person does, or if he is present in the worship service, on time at work, or haven't cheated on his spouse, which all of these are important. However, God measures faithfulness through obedience, or adherence to His Word. It is far more important men are obedient to God and His Word than how many times he was present in the worship service, or on the job.

Faithfulness causes a man to desire the things of God, to be in accordance with his commandments, and to abstain from that which has been noted in the Word of God.

Therefore, if one is faithful to Bible study, prayer service or the monthly meetings, but is not abstaining from fornication, lust, lies, cursing, adultery and every evil way; is he really faithful?

The Lord God is not going to measure your faithfulness based on your attendance in service, but your adherence to His Word and obedience is better than sacrifice.

Perfect

"Be ye therefore perfect, even as you're Father which is in heaven is perfect."
~Matthew 5:48 emphasis added

THE MAN LIKE GOD

This topic sends a proverbial shiver down almost everyone's spine when the conversation turns to perfection. We are happy to say we are perfectionist, but anyone professing that they are perfect risk being ostracized for this proclamation.

And yet the Lord, without hesitation or pause pronounces to the people of the day, that they should be perfect even as their Father in heaven is perfect.

First of all these people were not saved, had no Holy Ghost at the time and were at best ignorant of God's grace to even attempt to be so. And yet the Lord commanded them to be perfect.

Now, if it is not possible for man in the flesh to be perfect, why then would the Lord of all truth command us to be perfect?

Consider if you will, that Jesus already knew that many would take issue with this statement, and in their carnal minds would reject this command completely, choosing rather to remain imperfect in their minds even after the Lord had already made them perfect.

We consider Apostle Paul one of the most prolific Apostles of his day, and accept readily that he wrote letters to his recipients under the inspiration and direction of the Holy Ghost. Yet even Paul states in his writings:

"All scripture is given by inspiration of God, and is profitable for doctrine, for reproof, for correction, for instruction in righteousness: That the man of God may be perfect, thoroughly furnished unto all good works."

~2 Timothy 3:16-17

A Man Like God

Therefore, the message of perfection was reiterated through the teachings of Paul by the Holy Spirit, and cannot be disallowed simply because some don't believe in the ability of man; to be perfect in the flesh.

Many truly believe that because we can sin we can't be perfect, however, Jesus told the disciples to be perfect while they were yet sinners. Therefore, the ability to sin does not negate the commandment to be perfect.

Understanding Perfection

When the Lord commanded us to be perfect He was not speaking of being perfect by the flesh, or of fleshly means. It is through the Spirit of God perfection is reached, and it is only the Lord who can determine one's perfection.

One of the greatest mistakes we as saints make is in believing that because we can or do sin, we are again sinners.

If a man is born again, which means he has been cleansed of his sins, returns and sin again he is not again a sinner, but a backslider (if he continues in said sin and does not repent), God being married to the backslider. In this state he is a disobedient son, not a sinner again. Understanding that a sinner does not know he is sinning, a son does. Therefore, no saint or son of God is a sinner saved by grace.

Perfection then is a state in the Spirit of God, not a condition of the flesh as no good thing dwells in the flesh (see Romans 7:18). With this understanding a person who is an adulterer can be perfect, as David who

THE MAN LIKE GOD

was an adulterer, yet a perfect man as proclaimed by God.

Being perfect brings you to repentance when one does fall short. Perfection keeps one mindful of his responsibilities, and his promises. Because one who is perfect shall be like his God:

"The disciple is not above his master: but every one that is perfect shall be as his master."

~Luke 6:40

"Fear none of those things which thou shalt suffer: behold, the devil shall cast some of you into prison, that ye may be tried; and ye shall have tribulation ten days: be thou faithful unto death, and I will give thee a crown of life."

Revelations 2:10

APPENDIX

Glossary

Glossary

Abomination —An extreme hatred

Adam--The first man created by God upon earth. Hebrew word meaning man.

Adamic Curse—The curse placed upon Adam when he ate of the forbidden fruit in the Garden of Eden. All who have not received Jesus Christ as their personal Lord and Savior remain under this curse.

Adultery—Sexual intercourse with anyone other than one's spouse.

Catalyst—A person or thing that precipitates an event or change.

Clamour—A forcible expression of collective feeling or outrage.

Cleave —To adhere, cling, or stick fast. To be faithful.

Defile—To debase the pureness or excellence.

Denigrate—To attack the character or reputation.

Divorce—A state or country legal dissolving of a marriage between a husband and wife.

Dominion—To possess control over, as territory or sphere of influence.

Emulation—Effort or ambition to equal or surpass another.

Encumbered—To place a heavy burden on someone.

Envy—A feeling of discontent and resentment aroused by and in conjunction with desire for the possessions or qualities of another.

A Man Like God

Euphoria—A feeling of great happiness or well-being.

Eve—The first woman created and the wife of Adam. Meaning the mother of all.

Flesh—The carnal nature of man relating to God. Usually depicts someone who is not walking in the Spirit of God.

Forfeit—To surrender, to be deprived of, or give up the right to on account of a crime, an offense, an error, or a breach of contract.

Fornication—Any sexual act with a partner (male or female) outside of marriage between a man and a woman.

Frailties—A fault, especially a moral weakness.

Heresies—An opinion or a doctrine at variance with established religious belief against the Word of God.

Holy Ghost—The indwelling Spirit of God which comes down from Heaven and lives in the soul of a believer in Jesus Christ. Also known as the third person in the Trinity.

Holy Spirit—See Holy Ghost.

Homosexuality—Having sexual desires or orientation for members of the same sex.

Idiosyncrasies—A tendency, type of behavior, or mannerism.

Immorality—The quality of not being in accord with standards of right or good conduct.

Impede—To obstruct or block progress.

Glossary

Iniquity—Lack of justice or righteousness, wickedness, or injustice.

Jealousy—Suspicious or fearful of being displaced by a rival.

Kingdom—A territory, state, people, or community ruled or reigned over by a king or queen.

Lasciviousness—Giving to or expressing lust, exciting sexual desires.

Lust—Intense or unrestrained sexual craving.

Marriage—A binding vow between a man, woman, and God.

Masturbate—To stimulate the genital organs of oneself or another to achieve sexual pleasure.

Obliterate—To do away with completely so as to leave no trace.

Pernicious—Causing death or serious injury.

Pride—An excessively high opinion of oneself.

Pure Religion—To visit the fatherless and widows in their affliction, and to keep himself unspotted from the world.

Religion—A cause, principle, or activity pursued with zeal or conscientious devotion.

Repent—To feel such regret for past conduct as to change one's mind regarding it.

Revelry—Boisterous, noisy or unrestrained merrymaking.

A Man Like God

Sedition—Conduct or language inciting rebellion against God.

Sin—Disobedience to the known or unknown will of God.

Single—The state of having one mind, one thought, and one spirit. Not divided or broken.

Soul—The spiritual nature of humans regarded as immortal, separable from the body at death.

Undefiled—Having no faults; sinless.

Variance—The state or face of differing or of being in conflict. Discord.

Virgin—Male or female who have never experienced sexual intercourse.

Vitiates—To reduce the value or impair the quality, to corrupt morally; debase, to make ineffective.

Wrath—Forceful, often vindictive anger.

ABOUT THE AUTHOR

James Craig lives in Atlanta, GA, was born in 1964 the only child of his mother Miss Josie Bligen in Bronx, NY. He has two sons: Landon and Issac, one daughter named Shachia.

James is the founder of Raising Kingdom Citizens House of Worship, in Atlanta, GA, a small ministry dedicated to the uplifting of the Kingdom of Heaven.

James Craig has been chosen and mandated by God to re-establish kingdom principals and spiritual governmental authority in the earth. To bring forth a people prepared for the soon return of Christ, to build the true Church of Jesus Christ. To educate, reeducate, inspire, encourage, and empower the sons of God to move in their God-given authorities in the Earth Realm.

This is James sophomore project. His freshmen project: Black Sheep Secret: The Homosexual Spirit Exposed is available, and will be repackaged at a later date.

NOTES

NOTES

www.ingramcontent.com/pod-product-compliance
Lightning Source LLC
Chambersburg PA
CBHW061643040426
42446CB00010B/1556